Lean Game Development

Apply Lean Frameworks to the Process of Game Development

Second Edition

Julia Naomi Rosenfield Boeira

Apress®

Lean Game Development: Apply Lean Frameworks to the Process of Game Development, Second Edition

Julia Naomi Rosenfield Boeira
Winnipeg, MB, Canada

ISBN-13 (pbk): 978-1-4842-9842-8 ISBN-13 (electronic): 978-1-4842-9843-5
https://doi.org/10.1007/978-1-4842-9843-5

Managing Director, Apress Media LLC: Welmoed Spahr
Acquisitions Editor: Jessica Vakili
Development Editor: James Markham
Coordinating Editor: Spandana Chatterjee
Copy Editor: Kezia Endsley

Cover image from Freepik (www.freepik.com)

Distributed to the book trade worldwide by Apress Media, LLC, 1 New York Plaza, New York, NY 10004, U.S.A. Phone 1-800-SPRINGER, fax (201) 348-4505, e-mail orders-ny@springer-sbm.com, or visit www.springeronline.com. Apress Media, LLC is a California LLC and the sole member (owner) is Springer Science + Business Media Finance Inc (SSBM Finance Inc). SSBM Finance Inc is a **Delaware** corporation.

For information on translations, please e-mail booktranslations@springernature.com; for reprint, paperback, or audio rights, please e-mail bookpermissions@springernature.com.

Apress titles may be purchased in bulk for academic, corporate, or promotional use. eBook versions and licenses are also available for most titles. For more information, reference our Print and eBook Bulk Sales web page at http://www.apress.com/bulk-sales.

Any source code or other supplementary material referenced by the author in this book is available to readers on GitHub (https://github.com/Apress). For more detailed information, please visit https://www.apress.com/gp/services/source-code.

Paper in this product is recyclable

*To all women and non-binary folks who
work as game developers.*

Table of Contents

About the Author

 **Julia Naomi Rosenfield Boeira** has been a software engineer for almost two decades, focusing on game development, Rust, and online services. Currently, she works as a team lead at Ubisoft; previously she worked as tech lead engineer for an online service. She has also worked with premium Agile consultancy companies such as Thoughtworks and is extremely active on GitHub with a focus on game development and Rust.

Acknowledgments

This book would not have been possible without the support of my family: Diego, Kinjo, and Ffonxios; the contributions of Jay Kim, Evan Boehler, and Vitor Severo Leaes, who helped me review the book and gave me awesome feedback; to all the great Lean and Agile discussions I had with Paulo Caroli, Enzo Zuccoloto, and Marcelo Porcino at Thoughtworks; to the Rust in PoA Community: Julio, Douglas, Ruan, and Eva; to my parents who have always supported me and my studies; to my colleagues at Ubisoft: Evan, Denys, David, Madison, Poliana, Lune, Ryan N, Ryan H, Ryan F., Jesse M., and Sue; and, lastly, to my friends who helped me in this journey: Isabela Goes, Eva Pace, Thais Hamilton, Alexandra Perreira, Diego Ferreira, and Icaro Motta.

CHAPTER 1

Introduction

This book's goal is to present a new way of developing games to teams with little or no experience in Agile or Lean methodologies. In addition to that, this book uses a fictional game, which is the combination of three other anonymous games that were produced with the techniques presented in this book. Unfortunately, it is not possible to go into more detail about these games due to NDAs (agreements of secrecy).

Note The word *Lean* comes from the Toyota Production System, which is a systematic method for waste minimization without sacrificing productivity. Also, the concept of Lean was popularized by the book *The Lean Startup*, by Eric Ries, which aimed to create startup business models following five concepts, which are discussed later. This book specifically focuses heavily on Lean techniques from a game development point of view.

If you have some experience with game development, now is the time to put it aside. It's time to let go of the things you know and, with an open mind, learn something new, or at least from someone else's point of view. The goal of this book is to provide you with a game production model that prevents waste, reduces bugs, and offers continuous reviews. The book even offers a sequence of steps to eliminate unnecessary tasks. When I developed this methodology, I was thinking of small- to mid-sized game companies, but it can be used in large enterprises as well.

© Julia Naomi Rosenfield Boeira 2024
J. N. Rosenfield Boeira, *Lean Game Development*,
https://doi.org/10.1007/978-1-4842-9843-5_1

1

Besides that, I like to believe that this book is focused on small- to mid-sized *indie* game development companies—that is, perhaps, the group that would enjoy the most advantage by this methodology. Of course, large companies can also take advantage of the methodologies presented here; however, larger companies typically have more difficulty adapting these methodologies, since they have more bureaucratic processes, more vertical opinions, and more secrecy around their projects, making them more resistant to changes. In addition, they often need outside help to identify their strengths and weaknesses, as well as help to identify which points in the process are good or bad, since their more hierarchical nature usually prevents bottom-top improvements. Therefore, this book can be a tool for large companies in middleware projects, specific features, art, and tooling.

Why Lean Game Development, Not Agile Game Development?

Lean is something beyond Agile. In fact, many game companies have been unsuccessful in their first attempts to adopt Agile methodologies. This has generated some weird confusion about Scrum and Agile, which can be observed with tons of blog posts bashing Agile, mostly Scrum, for game development.

Another important factor is that many companies confuse Agile methodologies with Scrum, considering Scrum the only Agile tool available. The same happens with extreme programming (XP), and this confusion can have disastrous results. In fact, it's common to see companies adopting Scrums but not adopting the basic principles of Agile, which overloads the development teams. Another common case is those small "flexibilities" in the wrong direction of Scrum, which generate an even more waterfall process. How many times have I heard "This is not true Scrum!," "This is not really Agile," and "Now we have become Extreme Go Horse."[1]

Lean game development can meet the main needs of the game industry, but there are certain game-related aspects to take into account. For instance, game production is never 100 percent efficient, since you can't predict every possible problem, and it is far more difficult to find the "minimum" in a minimum viable product (MVP) in game development than in other industries. If you set fixed deadlines, the best you can expect is to get very close to them because unexpected problems and unexpected changes in scope will continue to happen, even after the deadlines. It's necessary to behave organically regarding changes, building in the ability to adapt to the environment.

Lean game development offers a methodological alternative to game development that can help you eliminate waste, get results as fast as possible, strengthen and empower teamwork, and get a better view of the whole work. How do you improve this visualization of the work? Kanban (which literally means a visualization card) is a classic tool that Lean development teams use.

That said, it's important to emphasize that in no way are Lean, Scrum, XP, or Kanban exclusive. They can be used together, thereby enjoying the best features of each.

---

[1]https://medium.com/@dekaah/22-axioms-of-the-extreme-go-horse-methodology-xgh-9fa739ab55b4

How Do Lean and Agile Relate to the Game World?

Lean game development is, above all, strongly inspired by Agile and can take advantage of Agile's tools to develop software. Therefore, let's look at the Agile Manifesto and interpret it to represent the vision of games. For such, I suggest the following point of view for games:

- *Individuals and interactions* over processes and tools
- *Games running* over comprehensive documentation[2]
- *Audience collaboration* over sales
- *Spontaneous development* over following a strict plan

Games and Software Relate Much More Deeply

To successfully understand Lean game development, you should first understand that digital games are also software and that software can be seen as a cooperative game of innovation and communication. Games are not only for children and teens; games are used to describe everything from romantic experiences to advanced military strategies, and they can also be used as another form of software development.

---

[2]www.gamedeveloper.com/disciplines/agile-game-development-part-3-working-game-vs-gdd

GAMES FOR MILITARY STRATEGIES

The Blitzkrieg board game was used for a long time to help train army officers. The game is set in World War II, in which two armies confront each other: Great Blue and Big Red. There are five countries, but the alliances are not built strictly and can vary depending on how the game is played.

The game has three modes: simple, advanced, and tournament. One of the most interesting aspects is that advanced mode offers many combat units, such as infantry, artillery, armored, assault, shots, bombing, and so on.

Unfortunately, the game is usually hard to find, maybe because it's old, and it usually takes a couple of days to finish gameplay. Figure 1-1 shows the (gigantic) board of the game with the different colored pieces.

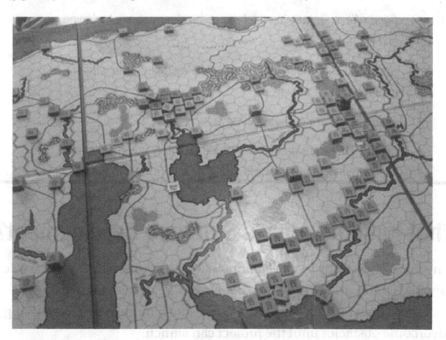

Figure 1-1. Avalon Hill's Blitzkrieg boardSource: boardgamegeek.com

When someone proposes to play a game, hundreds of alternatives come to mind: tic-tac-toe, checkers, chess, poker, 21, hide-and-seek, ping pong, and so on. Games usually fall into certain categories that help players realize how they are played and what the goals are.

- *Zero-sum*: These are games in which each user plays on an opposite side, and if one side wins, the other loses. Examples include checkers and tic-tac-toe.

- *Non-zero-sum*: These are games with multiple winners and losers. Examples include poker and hide-and-seek.

- *Positional*: These are games where the overall state of the game can be determined by looking at the board. Examples include chess and tic-tac-toe.

- *Competitive*: Games in which there's a clear notion of winning and losing.

- *Cooperative*: In these games, people play together to win, or until they find it necessary.

- *Finite*: These are games that have an end.

- *Infinite*: These are games where the primarily intention is to keep playing. In other words, the goal is to remain in the game.

What Kind of Game Is Software Development?

Many people see software development as a positional game, with a cycle of small victories and a clear goal. But a software development game is much more than positions on a board and much more than a team trying to overcome obstacles until the project can launch.

Software development is a cooperative game, in which all pieces must help each other in order to reach each one of the goals. Think of a survival game, in which each member of the team has a specific and unique skill that is useful to the group's survival. The software development process is similar to the concept of a cooperative game. There should be no leader; instead, a group of people unite to make the best decisions and divide tasks the best way possible to survive (win).

Where Did We Go Wrong?

Unfortunately, over time, people got the idea that stricter and heavier methodologies, with more control and more artifacts, would be "safer" for a project's development. However, no one likes to play games with hundreds of rules that need to be remembered every minute in order for the player to perform correctly.

The best games are those that can be played in a relaxed way so that if a rule is broken, there won't be any big consequences for the result. Furthermore, games that allow the player to be creative and imaginative tend to provide much more cooperation. You just have to observe kids playing board games to realize this.

Taking this into consideration, why not apply this to software development? Let's look at an example of the negative effect that rigidity and heaviness can have on the classic board game Monopoly. Imagine that, besides the players, you have a person solely responsible for administering the bank, one for administering the real estate, another one for administering the real estate bank, one for administrating your life (chance cards), one police officer for administering prisons and the flow of characters, another one to roll the dice, and so on.

This type of model is the software development model used in most companies: it's highly hierarchical, it has several types of control over individuals, it has strict rules, micromanagement is encouraged, it's difficult to play, and it's aimed at exploring others. How can this model be superior to a relaxed, fun, creative, and cooperative model? The Agile Manifesto, the framework, and the methodology should not be applied in a rigid and immutable way. After all, a game should allow for fun, cooperation, and creativity.

Probably, this presumption that heavier methodologies are safer comes from the assumption that project managers can't look at the code and evaluate the degree of development, the status, and the project situation. Adding weight and rigidity to the model won't make the fear and insecurity regarding the project better, however. In fact, the consequence will be making your team delay their work and miss the deadline.

To achieve satisfactory results, always keep in mind that developing software is a team game, in which the production manager is not superior to anyone else. Remember, there are ways to document while the code is being written, and there are ways to visualize the software development without increasing the pressure on the team. A production manager shouldn't think of the team as people to boss around and coordinate, but rather as colleagues that they need to help.

The following are some prejudices of the game industry regarding the Agile methodology[3]:

- Test automation in games is much more complex than in other software industries.

- The game visual aspect cannot be tested automatically.

- Making open betas and demos for kids to test the game is much cheaper.

- The current business model in the sector is based on feature-complete games.

- "I don't like Scrum," because Scrum was the answer to Agile methodologies.

- The game's sequences and sequels are not iterations.

---

[3] www.gamedeveloper.com/programming/agile-game-development-is-hard

- Art cannot be iterated, and games are art.

- Games are developed so that the users play longer, not to save time like in e-commerce.

- It is impossible to create an automated test pyramid for games, especially large productions.

- From a production's point of view, continuous delivery is not attractive to games.

All of these points are discussed in depth in later chapters, but I think it's important to point out now why each of them is wrong:

- Test automation may be more complex, but it is certainly as or more valuable than in other industries.

- Gameplay tests and tests that identify errors in images, as well as how close an image is to ideal, are fundamental features for games. These kinds of tests are regularly done in mobile development and frontend development. For games, we have a few resources that can help measure this, like OpenCV.

- Having children test games, even if it generates some degree of satisfaction in them, is morally wrong and can greatly affect the reception of a game. If they are your target audience, be sure to have parents involved.

- Scrum most definitely is not the only Agile methodology.

- Later, you will see that art is a creative and iterative process.

- You want users to play longer, but spend less time trying to learn the game, where and when to click, and its mechanics.

- Not only is it possible to test games, I wrote a book on automated testing for games.

- In the old days, when the game came in a cartridge and there was no Internet to update the game, this phrase could even make sense. Nowadays, some games are released without even being ready.

Thus, it's important to understand the basics of Lean and remind yourself that software development is a cooperative and fun game, in which all pieces are important. It's a game that always produces more knowledge. Ideally, it must be managed organically and with low hierarchy to prevent waste (of human potential, of time, of excessive documentation, of conflicts, of stress, etc.).

This book covers several aspects of Lean development—such as the basic aspects, the inception, and MVPs—and applies them to games. You also learn how to use test-driven development, how to use continuous integration in games, and how to generate hypotheses. Lastly, you see how design and build[4] are different and learn more about tests, measurement and analysis, and the generation of ideas.

Summary

In this chapter, I talked about the relationship of Lean and Agile in the game development world. I also discussed the deeper relationship that games and software have, including how software development can be seen as a game.

---

[4] A general reference to software engineering and its practices.

CHAPTER 2

First Steps with Lean

This chapter explains Lean in a deeper sense and how it relates to game development. It also presents a visualization of the Lean game development cycle. Finally, the chapter introduces some places where Lean game development can take advantage of Agile methodologies.

Seven Key Principles of Lean

When starting to talk about Lean in more detail, it's important to cover the seven key principles of Lean:

- *Eliminate waste*: This includes avoiding the following: producing disorderly and unnecessary inventory and requirements, giving excessive importance to defects that don't affect the user experience, processing unnecessary information, and creating long wait times. To reach those goals, avoid unnecessary code and features. Another important consideration is to not start more activities than can be completed.

  From a business point of view, it's necessary to elaborate on the requirements so they are easily understood and to avoid changing them constantly. Especially avoid bureaucracy. Inefficient communication can lead to misunderstandings

© Julia Naomi Rosenfield Boeira 2024
J. N. Rosenfield Boeira, *Lean Game Development*,
https://doi.org/10.1007/978-1-4842-9843-5_2

regarding the job to be done. From a developer's point of view, it's important to ensure that the job is complete and that you don't end up with defects and quality issues in the finished code. But maybe the most important issue is to prevent unnecessary changes in the job tasks.

- *Build with quality*: Quality problems lead to waste; in addition, it's a waste to test something more than once. To avoid quality problems, you can use pair programming and test-driven development. Both are fundamental tools, and both are e described in the coming chapters of this book.

- *Generate knowledge*: Generate knowledge while you're working so that the whole team can follow the software development process and have the technical ability to deal with problems. A usual way to generate knowledge is through pair programming and code reviews. Wikis, dev huddles, and docs are other tools you can use to share knowledge.

- *Postpone commitment*: Complex solutions should not be treated rashly, and irreversible decisions should not be made hastily.

- *Deliver fast*: It's common for people to spend a lot of time thinking about requirements that may or may not come up. Workers can also become mentally blocked or start thinking of solutions with excessive engineering. You can avoid this problem by gathering the right people, keeping things simple, and using teamwork.

- *Respect people*: The workplace should be pleasant, so never forget to be courteous with people. No matter what your position is in the company, you must always seek for equity between roles.

- *Optimize the whole*: This principle seems simple and intuitive, but it's usually not taken into account. It's important to identify failures, propose solutions to them, and look for feedback. A whole is not made solely by its parts but by people interacting.

While using the following methodologies, it's always important to keep these Lean principles in mind.

Lean Inception

An interesting stage of software development in the Lean methodology is the Lean inception. Briefly, the *inception* is a workshop, done typically in a week, with many activities of alignment and goal setting. The product evolution ends up being represented by a minimum viable product (MVP) and a sequence of iterations over the MVP, each with its own features. If the team has enough time, defining alternative MVPs in case of failure is also a nice strategy.

The main goal is to define the scope of what is being created so that the team has a clear view of the path to follow, that is, the minimum game that needs to be built to generate results and verify its viability. If an MVP proves to be non-viable, new MVPs can be generated. Figure 2-1 provides insight into an MVP and its sequences. The MVP 1 part corresponds to the people who are going to prove that your MVP is worth it, known as early adopters. They will cut their own grass with the best tool available, while MVP 8 will allow people to cut the grass in a football field.

Another important point to learn from Figure 2-1 is that the MVP is not only about how feasible or how valuable the product is, but how delightful and usable is. When considering an MVP, you need to add elements from all of these aspects (feasibility, value, delightfulness, and usability). Another, more recent, idea is the MLP (Minimum Lovable Product), which differentiates itself from an MVP by focusing on delivering something that is more effective in an already saturated market.[1]

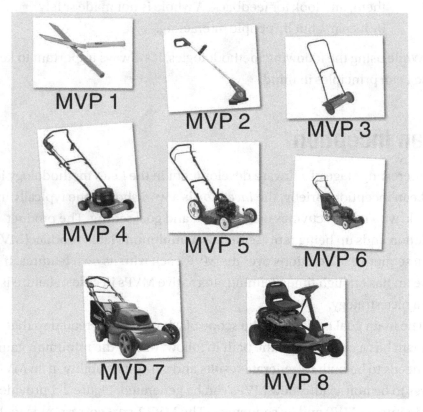

Figure 2-1. MVPs must occur incrementally, so that each increment provides a new return. Source: https://caroli.org/en/mvp-examples

---

[1]https://medium.com/codica/what-is-a-minimum-lovable-product-and-how-to-build-one-22cb61f67e8a

MVP CANVAS

The MVP canvas gathers elements from design thinking, Lean startup, and business directives. It's a template to validate new ideas and question existing ones. It's divided into seven branches.

MVP vision: What product vision must this MVP deliver?

Metrics for hypothesis validation: How do you measure the results of this MVP? And from what business point of view?

Outcome statement: What knowledge are you seeking with this MVP?

Features: What do you intend to build with this MVP? Which actions can be taken in order to simplify the MVP?

Personas and platforms: For whom is this MVP?

Journeys: Which user journeys will be improved in this MVP?

Cost and schedule: What are the cost and schedule for this MVP?

Read more at www.caroli.org/.

How Does Lean Inception Apply to Games?

The main tasks of the Lean inception are to come up with the game features, its basic game design, and the tools to be used. In short, there's a whole series of possible applications of the inception. It's also important to get the whole team engaged to increase motivation and build empowerment in the group. A more horizontal team is more engaged, has more respect for what is being developed, and enjoys a greater sense of ownership over the product.

Lean PMO

The *project management office* (PMO) is a group of people (or even a single individual) responsible for keeping an integrated vision of the strategic plan throughout the whole product development, including managing deadlines, project rescoping, and costs. These people are responsible for gathering the company's portfolio to guide, plan, and organize the activities of the projects in the best way possible.

A Lean PMO manages the game development and organizes and keeps track of requests and MVPs. The PMO does this by taking into consideration the body of work, without getting mired in Agile technical details, like with what can happen with extreme programming (XP), Scrum, and Kanban.

The PMO's main role is to guarantee the continuous delivery of the game. This person/group needs to be aware of the whole and not the details and periodically monitor the product development.

How Does a Lean PMO Apply to Games?

When it comes to game development, the Lean PMO is usually the team that gives the go-ahead for a game to move to the next stage, release an open beta or demo, or the game launch itself. This may vary when considering the company size, as larger companies tend to have more steps and be less Lean. Talking about continuous delivery when the game is not yet on the market might seem like shooting yourself in the foot, but continuous delivery doesn't necessarily have to be for the gamer. The idea behind this is managing the development steps, so that the product continues to evolve and receive feedback.

Lean DevOps

The function of *DevOps* is to connect the practices of DevOps to the Lean MVP perspective (which is explained in the next chapter). DevOps refers to the practices that the team uses while creating and delivering the game.

DevOps doesn't have to be executed by a single person; it can be used by a group of people, by different people in different moments, and in different practical activities. It includes working with features and user stories. Some teams have specific people on the project who lead DevOps initiatives, such as the tool team.

How Does Lean DevOps Apply to Games?

You can, for instance, designate people who are responsible for organizing and applying the techniques, methodologies, and tools that the team has, as well as guiding the game's deployment.

Kanban

Kanban is based on Toyota's just-in-time model. The method consists of visualizing the workflow and acting on the process in order to not overload the members of the team. The process is exposed to the team members using the visual management approach, from the early stages to the final delivery.

Physical or virtual boards can be used, such as Trello. Some Kanbans are divided into columns and rows, but not all of them need to be. There are some very creative implementations; just search for and use the one that matches your team's needs.

A Kanban is composed of several "cards," with each one representing an action that must be taken. The action's degree of completion is marked on a panel, usually called the *Heijunka board*. This system has some advantages; it's easy to identify waste and can lead to faster cycles that increase productivity. When associated with virtual boards and processes, collecting information about cycles is very efficient; in the case of physical boards, it depends on the feeling and expertise of each team.

Color coding can indicate the status of the card and enable people to identify delays, allowing them to be solved first. Different cards in the same zone usually mean a failing flow and must be resolved. Many companies automate parts of the process with light signals on machines/user stories that are struggling with certain tasks. I worked with a developer experience team that developed an internal tool connecting Jira with Grafana to alert teams about user stories that they were struggling with.

From my point of view, this helps eliminate long daily meetings, as the board state is visible to everyone; the need of a Scrum Master, as blockers are visible and transparent to the whole team; and other wastes. Laborious tasks can often be divided into smaller ones, also increasing efficiency.

The work-in-progress (WIP) concept is used to limit activities that will be "pulled" in the Kanban method. From the Kanban's point of view, the next activity is only pulled when the WIP has work capacity. The WIP restrictions identify bottlenecks and possible problem areas in the process, helping to make team decisions (you can read more at www.caroli.org/).

A common concept to deal with work that is blocked is to label the task with a Blocked tag or label to communicate flow issues to the team and leadership—and, if necessary, take on another task until the blockage is resolved.

How Can You Take Advantage of Scrum?

As you probably know, *Scrum* is an Agile framework for completing and managing complex projects. It is highly recommended for projects that have requirements that change rapidly.

Its progression happens through iterations called *sprints*, which usually last from one to four weeks, but can last as long as necessary to complete the selected tasks (or until they are reprioritized). The model suggests that each sprint starts with a planning meeting and ends with a review on the work done. So, it consists of short and cadenced cycles, with alignment meetings to monitor the work evolution and team efficiency.

Other stages, such as the retrospective and grooming stages, must be considered keywords. Typically, they correspond to team ceremonies that aim to review the steps and plan the next ones.

In this framework, there are often meetings called *stand-ups*, usually called *dailies* in other frameworks. Stand-ups allow the team to check on the progress, communicate blockers, ask for help, and be transparent over the task progression. In these meetings, all the team members stand up and answer three questions: "What did I do yesterday?" and "What am I going to do today?" and "What is blocking me?" The answers to those questions feed the team's reflection, re-orientation, and decision-making.

Using Scrum encourages the empowerment of a multifunctional and self-organized team. The team's efficiency depends on its ability to work together. The team should not have a leader, and everyone should help make decisions.

SCRUM KEYWORDS

Here are some important terms to know:

Scrum Master. This is a person familiar with the framework, whose goal is to facilitate the team in the Scrum process. It can be anyone from the development team. I find that teams without set Scrum Masters work better together, because the Scrum Master changed during every sprint.

Product owner. This is a representative of the company, of the clients, or of the users. This person guides the team on the product's vision. The person must lead the development effort through explanations and priority setting.

Continuous Integration

Continuous integration is a software development practice in which team members frequently integrate their code. Each integration is verified through automated tests that detect integration errors quickly. Other tools—such as formatting, linting, and dependency checks—can be used with each integration.

Integration assumes a high level of automated testing. You learn more about continuous integration in Chapter 8, but the most common tools for games are Game.CI, GitHub Actions, CircleCI, and Jenkins.

From Build-Measure-Learn to Lean Game

This section briefly presents some steps of the Lean software development process. You can adapt the steps shown in Figure 2-2 for game development, but the central idea is to generate ideas, build concepts, code, measure, get data, learn with data, and generate new ideas, all in a continuous loop.

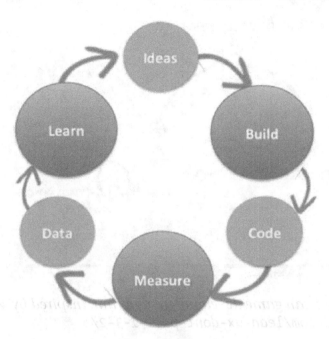

Figure 2-2. *Build-measure-learn diagram. Source:* `www.caroli.org/` `what-to-build`

Figure 2-3 shows the outcome of Figure 2-2 when applied to the game development process.

LEAN GAME DEVELOPMENT

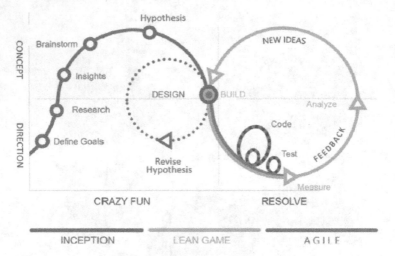

Figure 2-3. *Lean game development diagram. Inspired by:* www.
lithespeed.com/lean-ux-dont-part-1-3-2/

The following steps summarize the process shown in Figure 2-3:

1. *Inception*: The concept is set at the Lean inception
   stage. It comprises a series of substeps, as follows:

   a. *Define goal*: The team gathers to build the ideas on which the
      inception is going to be based.

   b. *Research*: The team gets information on the possibilities
      allowed by the goals.

   c. *Give insights*: These are moments of inspiration, when team
      members aim to "think outside the box."

   d. *Brainstorm*: This is when you expose your creativity. Don't be
      afraid of your ideas. The more absurd, the better.

   e. *Make hypotheses*: This moment allows teams to turn all ideas
      into measurable goals.

2. *Design*: In my opinion, this is one of the most interesting moments because it's when the game comes alive.

    a. *Revise hypotheses*: With the current game design, you can do the first measurement, which consists of determining whether the hypotheses created are proper in the context.

3. *Build*: Here you define what is possible to do and how to do it.

    a. *Code*: Develop the art, animation, code, models, and so on.

    b. *Test*: Get the initial feedback of what is being done, especially if it's automated.

4. *Measure*: With the build ready, you must measure the impact of the game. There are many ways to do this, but feedback from the community is a great way to start.

5. *Analyze*: You get an understanding of everything that was measured.

6. *Iterate*: With Lean, it's always important to iterate to generate new ideas, concepts, features, and knowledge. To iterate means to start again.

One thing you can see in the Lean Game Development diagram is the presence of Agile as part of Lean. This is not necessarily a precise concept, but a metaphor that represents different concepts that can run in parallel. Agile methodologies promote the idea of building better products with better quality that focus on people. Lean, on the other hand, promotes the workflow, focusing on products that bring more value to the customers, in order to continuously improve products and processes. Fortunately, both can be easily coordinated, as they involve quick interactions and seek feedback for improvement. This is probably why Scrum vs Lean arguments are common, as Scrum seems to go a bit into the Lean territory.

Looking Deeper at the Inception

The inception is a useful activity to kick-start a project and define the user stories. At this stage, here are the important questions:

- What are the project's goals?

- Who is going to use this system?

- What are the roles each team member will perform in the game development?

Once you set some goals, the team can start to develop the journeys from the personas (you learn about the concept of personas in the next chapter), using the following sequence: *As X, I want Y and, therefore, Z, so what does X want from the system in order to get Z?* From the answers to these questions, the team can create stories on which the software must be based.

How Does It Apply to Games?

As in other examples, the model is not perfect for games because there are some ideas missing. How can you adapt and improve this model? I suggest asking the following questions:

- What is the game's narrative?

- What is the central characteristic of the game?

- What do you want to achieve with this game?

- What kind of user are you aiming for?

- How can the user play the new game?

- What uncertainties does this project have in its future?

As you answer these questions, you can determine the players' journeys, as shown here:

- As X, I want to be able to do Y; therefore, I want Z.

- So, what does X want to do in the game to get Z?

Also, remember that the game design process, which is a very complicated topic on its own, also needs to be iterated and developed. No game starts with a feature complete game design document, and no group delivers a game that resembles the original GDD. Most of them start with a box cover pitch or a single-page design pitch, then that pitch gradually evolves into a ten-page design document. Right before the team enters full production, they have something that looks like a game design document. If game design is an area of interest, I recommend the book *Level Up,* from Scott Rogers.

Test-Driven Development

Test-driven development (TDD) avoids problems by proposing to write tests before developing code. *If developers know how the game is tested, they are more likely to think through all test scenarios before coding*, which can greatly improve code design. Here are the most common steps of TDD:

1. Write the test.

2. Run the test and see it fails.

3. Write the code.

4. Run the test to see if it works.

5. Refactor.

6. Iterate.

Chapters 10, 15, and 16 focus on the TDD process, especially regarding games.

Lean and Games

With all this basic knowledge, it is possible to superficially understand what Lean is and some applications of it to games. You can now think about the first step to understanding Lean game development—an inception, for example. This is a good time to reflect on what the figures presented in this chapter can teach you and what steps you should take.

Summary

In this chapter, I reviewed the seven key principles of Lean development. I briefly introduced Lean practices and how they apply to games. Finally, I showed how the Lean game development cycle can make the development process richer with a few Agile concepts.

CHAPTER 3

An Inception in Practice

The previous chapter explained what an inception is; in this chapter, you see why it's so important. Often, before starting a project, team members don't know each other. Thus, one of the functions of an inception is to increase team rapport. There are several techniques, called *ice breakers,* to help with this.

With that resolved, you'll move on to topics such as goal setting, game scoping and strategies, feature mapping, and prioritization. These techniques are the basis of this chapter.

Inception Defined

The way I conceive an inception is inspired by what Paulo Caroli describes in his blog (http://www.caroli.org).

© Julia Naomi Rosenfield Boeira 2024
J. N. Rosenfield Boeira, *Lean Game Development,*
https://doi.org/10.1007/978-1-4842-9843-5_3

HOW TO MODEL AN INCEPTION

Usually, you can follow this simple model:

- The inception lasts from one to five days, depending on the game's complexity and the necessity.
- You count on the presence of the entire development team—publishers, producers, coordinators, and other parties interested in the game's success.

- A "war room" is booked for the inception for as long as it's necessary (preferably, so that the "mess" remains).

- Having lots of colored sticky notes will allow you to do lots of brainstorming.

- Have people prepare their ideas for the brainstorming before the actual brainstorm meeting.

- You can find more information about inceptions at the following locations:

- www.caroli.org/back-to-the-basics-what-made-this-agile-inception-especial/

- www.caroli.org/user-stories-and-business-hypothesis/

- https://caroli.org/en/lean-inception-learn-how-to-align-people-and-build-the-right-product/

Anatomy of an Inception

This section explains some concepts based on examples. A fictional game will be revealed bit by bit to give you a sense of progression along with the knowledge being gained. (The game presented here is generated from a combination of multiple games with their NDA sections removed.) The problem was how do we develop a computer game, our passion, in order to make the most of the techniques we use in day-to-day Agile and Lean software development, based on our personal preferences. We wanted to create a game development model that would allow other game companies to develop their products more profitably, with shorter iteration and feedback cycles, and higher quality and greater certainty of success. We needed to start somewhere—the *inception*! We gathered people interested in the studio project and started thinking.

Our inception was attended by some people from outside the game development team, since it was small. It lasted approximately one day, but its stages were closed during the week with the development team and some outside people who were called in for specific meetings. Thus, processes such as defining objectives and research were already partially underway, so we held a session to prioritize the defined objectives.

The following sections focus on the ideation stage of the inception, which consists of defining objectives and insights and then brainstorming and generating hypotheses, as depicted in Chapter 2's Lean game development diagram.

Defining Goals

Objectives are goals that the team defines as priorities to achieve what is expected from the game. *Insights* are an understanding of the game needs, respecting its goals, in order to generate clear ideas on how to achieve these desired goals—an epiphany of narrative and art in the context of games.

Researching

We asked all the team members to research games available on the market and the general public's interest in games. We also asked each team member to share their gaming interests and experience. This helped create a benchmark for what the game should be.

Generating Insights

This stage is for reaching an understanding of the game's needs and respecting its goals so the team can generate clear ideas on how to reach those desired goals. It's an epiphany of narrative and art in the context of games.

Insights are different from brainstorming. The insights represent an understanding of ways to achieve the objectives and often serve as the basis for brainstorming, which aims to generate ideas about what was established with the insights and in the objectives.

We presented the ideas that were most relevant and most fun to the development of the game. The next block represents examples of responses that were obtained during the session.

The Game's Narrative

Here is the game's narrative:

- It's a *Mario*-like game (following 2D platform game style).

- The character Jujuba faces enemies from a gang (*Streets of Rage*).

- Marcibal and the Xandra gang kidnap people to perform satanic rituals.

- It's a post-apocalyptic world.

- There are hidden and explosive things (*Bomberman*).

- Who doesn't like cats and bombs? (*Exploding Kittens*)

- There are stun guns (*Super Shock*).

- Kamehamehaaaaaa! (boss fight mode like in *Dragon Ball Budokai*).

The Game's Main Characteristics

These are the main characteristics of the game:

- It's a 2D platform.

- Characters can walk, jump, and fall (gameplay mechanics).

- Characters can die and be reborn (that is, they have several lives).

- Characters can kill enemies and evil kidnappers (gameplay fun).

The Game's Intended Outcome

These are the game's intended outcomes:

- To prove that Lean game development can be used for game development.

- To prove that small projects can enjoy a lot of the advantages of Agile and Lean methodologies.

- To provide a lot of fun and learning.

- The objective of one of the original games was to mobilize the studio for a new creative process.

The Game's Intended Audience

This is the game's intended audience:

- Players who want to have fun with an immersive game.

- Players who like to focus on fast games (games that can easily save progress).

- Players who like to focus on games with increasing difficulty levels.

How Are Users Able to Play?

This is how users can play:

- Moves are restricted to the keyboard, namely, the arrow keys, the spacebar, and the A, S, D, W keys.

- Will there be a video game joystick?

- There are no external resources.

Project Uncertainties

What was unknown at the beginning of the project:

- Uncertainty about the Lean process for games.

- Difficulty choosing the game platform.

- Publishing process defined by the publisher.

Prioritizing Ideas

After you gather all your ideas, it's necessary to prioritize them, so you can focus on the ideas you want to demonstrate first. We did this as follows:

- Each person builds their favorite sequence (in case of the game narrative, we chose to order the three favorite). When everyone is done, the classification is exposed.

- Using the sequence generated by the preference classification (preferential vote system), we created a board containing the sequences in each of the items.

- From these sequences, we created action items that again were voted on and ordered, but this time they're all in the same group.

- The items are used in a discussion to define which ones have priority and which ones are easier to solve first.

- With these action items, we generated the minimum viable products (MVPs) described in the next chapter, the personas, and the user journeys.

Developing Personas

Personas are a way for the team to visualize the profiles of its main users, while developing the game and during the inception (see Figure 3-1). They gather attributes such as personal interests, age, job, hobbies, and so on.

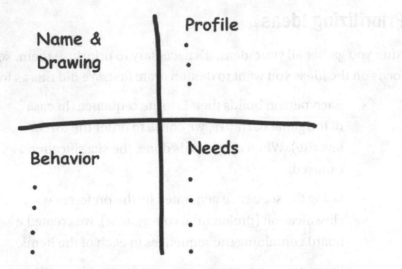

Figure 3-1. *Natalia Arsand's personas template. Source:*
`www.caroli.org/atividade-identificando-personas`

Follow these steps when creating personas:

1. Ask the inception members to divide into pairs
   or small groups, and then deliver the personas
   template shown in Figure 3-1 to each group.

2. Ask each group to create a persona, using the
   template as a reference.

3. Ask the participants to present their personas to the
   whole team.

4. Ask the team to switch groups and repeat
   Steps 1 to 3.

At the end of the activity, a group of personas have been created, and
the different types of game users have been described. The stakeholders
who know the project's goals must participate actively in the activity,
helping the team to create the personas and suggesting changes to their
descriptions, as needed. Furthermore, many of the ideas that came up at

the inception can be used here, proving the need for previous research on the game. (For more information, see www.romanpichler.com/blog/10-tips-agile-personas/ and www.caroli.org/new-talk-user-story-a-holistic-view/.)

It is important to remember that defining personas at this stage is not definitive, but an initial construction. These can and should be iterated, rethought, and changed with each iteration.

Journeys of Personas

The following persona wish list was copied exactly as it was developed during the inception for our *Mario*-like game:

- Like Carlita, I want to be able to make the "princess" save the day; therefore, I want the *main character to be a girl*.

- Like Rodrigo, I want to be able to play for hours. Therefore, I want a *different game experience in each level*.

- Like Thais, I want the enemies to be real and personified; therefore, I want them to be based on *real and credible situations*.

- Like Guilherme, I want the *game to remind me of the old days* of video games; therefore, I want an experience like *Mario* 2.0.

Note that the idea of personas is to define which scope of priorities is important for each persona or group of personas, which makes it easier to focus on the target audience and sub-target audiences.

Stories

This is the stage where you extract the art concepts, features, mechanics, and user experience (UX) from the personas. These stories are not necessarily tasks or stories in the practical Kanban sense, but more akin to epics and initiatives:

- Carlita wants Jujuba to be a *strong character* and, like in *Frozen*, wants the plot to be about sisters.

- Like Rodrigo, I want *every level to present new challenges*, such as new enemies and new skills.

- Thais wants the characters to produce a *sense of familiarity and/or humanity*.

- In Guilherme's opinion, it's important to at least be able to *jump, walk,* and *fall*.

Brainstorming

The following is a paraphrased series of rules designed to produce a more productive brainstorming session. These were taken from Gabriel Albo of ThoughtWorks and were inspired by the ideas proposed in *7 Tips on Better Brainstorming* (OPENIDEO, 2011).

- *Have one conversation at a time.* Avoid side conversations, as they often blur the inception objectives.

- *Try to create as many* ideas as possible. The purpose of brainstorming is to generate ideas, so quantity matters. Try to write down everything that crosses your mind—it's worth taking inspiration from other people's ideas too.

- Build ideas over others' ideas. Using other people's ideas as inspiration mainly helps to start the ideation process, but it can also have a very cool consequence: that of containing a possible narrative of ideas.

- Encourage crazy ideas. No idea is bad or crazy. In the context of an inception, bold ideas can differentiate a really innovative game.

- Be visual. Write the ideas; if necessary, make drawings. In addition, it is important to organize ideas by context.

- Maintain the focus. Focus is important to ensure a successful session. In very creative environments, loss of focus can cause a drift that is very difficult to recover from.

- *Don't criticize or judge.* Don't criticize bold, simple, or crazy ideas. All ideas are welcome and can offer unique approaches.

Modern Brainstorming

Traditional brainstorming often excludes the ideas of introverts and quiet people, as the meeting tends to demand people to voice and give context to their ideas. The result is that "group think" can dominate the session, and only one approach is explored.

More modern brainstorming concepts[1] focus on the fact that introverts are not necessarily heard and that individuals might be able to contribute more if they have their own brainstorming session. From these individual sessions, start small group sessions to try to converge ideas. Once the first session has mostly converged, you can switch people around to get fresh perspectives and iterate more on the concept. The rule here is no criticism.

---

[1] A Better Way to Brainstorm: How to Get Students to Generate Original Ideas
https://www.youtube.com/watch?v=GLpZ6RZHyoM

Once enough of these sessions have occurred, you can have a centralized session, where each group has the opportunity to share ideas and debate for a rich convergence.

Creating Hypotheses

Lean hypotheses are the main way a team can guide and evolve the development of the game. With generated hypotheses, an MVP can be elaborated on and use the hypotheses as validators.

Chapters 4 and 5 cover MVPs and hypotheses in more detail.

The Game, from the Inception Point of View

We will create a 2D platform game in which the character Jujuba must survive a series of challenges to rescue her sister Xuxuba from the hands of the evil Marcibal, a member of the Xandra gang.

Summary

In this chapter, you learned how an inception works and what kind of information you can get from it, such as narratives, aesthetics, and game features, as well as your goals, your users, and basic mechanics. You also saw how to prioritize ideas generated in an inception and how to develop personas that will guide you through development.

With this information in hand, you identify the features that the game must present and an idea of their sequence. From this moment on, the concept of MVPs emerges, as well as how to prioritize them.

The next chapter gets into the details of how to build the MVPs and the user journey, as well as how personas and hypotheses are extracted and used so that they generate the concepts of value of delivery (MVPs) and validation of delivery (hypotheses).

CHAPTER 4

MVPs: Do We Really Need Them?

In this chapter, you learn what a minimum viable product (MVP) is and how it can be applied to game development. The chapter also covers how to deliver your game prototypes for validation and how to apply MVP canvas concepts to prioritize your prototypes. Finally, you learn how these concepts are developed in a real project.

MVP and MVG Defined

A *minimum viable product* (MVP) is a minimum set of essential features necessary to have a functional product that delivers value to a business (minimum product) and that can also be used by the end consumer (viable product). It works incrementally so that each new MVP/increment delivers the next set of minimum features, allowing the product to constantly increase in value.

The concept of MVP is not so simple when it comes to games because in most cases companies want to deliver a finished and complete game, and their clients want the same. Therefore, you need a *minimum viable game* (MVG), in short, the minimum vertical slice of your game. However, it's necessary to remember that a minimum viable game must contain some value. An MVG is a wrapper expression for an MVP in the gaming industry. MVGs can be interoperable, but as you see in this chapter, an MVG demands a little for being viable, and the delivery methods are not necessarily for the end user.

When developing, you need to determine how your game is unique. What quality makes it unique? Are all the features necessary? Is it necessary to develop everything from scratch, or are there tools to help with the development? Do these tools satisfy all your requirements? Do you have the necessary feedback for your idea? Is your team integrated?

At this point, you need to understand these two distinct concepts:

- *MVP*: Defines the moment in which the game is presentable to the client (even as a demo).

- *The prototype*: An internal step needed to define the minimal development to achieve a valuable business result.

When you develop games, especially those with new features, it's necessary to keep in mind that game development is made of prototypes of features and mechanics. No one starts developing a game with advanced features, complete animation, and perfect art. Usually, a prototype looks something like Figure 4-1, in other words, something similar to a 3D Atari game.

Figure 4-1. *Example of a 3D prototype. Source: New York Film Academy (www.nyfa.edu/student-resources/getting-the-most-out-of-your-prototype-game)*

Building Prototypes

The goal of a prototype is to find problems during the development process. You don't want a blocking bug in the game that surprises the client while they are having fun.

These disturbances are common in racing games, for instance, when the player jumps higher than expected and the car gets stuck inside the mountain. To help overcome this obstacle, the MVG has several prototypes (as many as necessary), each with a single feature, a single implemented mechanic, a minimal set of innovations, and/or new art/animation. That is, a prototype has the ultimate goal of testing an idea.

Don't try to implement thousands of things at once; your emotional well-being will thank you. An MVG is simply a generic concept that describes the minimum set of prototypes that must be assembled to make your game commercially viable. A prototype is the minimum set of features that must be developed in order to deliver value and test an idea. Another difference is that an MVG involves delivering value to the customer, while prototyping generally delivers value to the business.

The PO's Role in MVPs/Prototypes

You know that an MVP/prototype needs a product owner (PO). Who can be the team's PO? Who can be the person in charge of ensuring that the game's development is in sync with the desired vision? When you think of POs, you probably make associations with the idea of Scrum. But ask yourself whether this association is the only way to go. In some game studios, POs are often referred to as directors (technical, design, gameplay, art). It all depends on the size of the production. The producer can act as the PO.

When a game is being developed, it's easy for the team to spend years developing a new game each quarter. Remember the game *FEZ*, featured in the documentary *Indie Game: The Movie*? It was an amazing game, which me and my son played for hours. However, the game creator, designer, and developer was also the PO, the person responsible for guaranteeing the game's vision. This duplicity of roles meant the game took years to launch, and consequently, this had a negative impact on the product marketing.

The PO must be someone who understands how the users and the market are going to behave. In most times, the PO doesn't have to be someone in the company but someone who can make small suggestions to ensure the integrity and correct vision of the product. It should be someone capable of setting the most important features and, preferably, someone who can follow the development of the game at all stages.

Another important function of the PO is to determine when prototypes have been validated or MVGs have been achieved. For example, a good MVG concept is to release alphas and betas, as with Minecraft. Minecraft is one of the most successful indie games of recent times and its market impact has been huge (I myself have spent hours playing with my son).

What, then, are good prototypes and minimum viable products when it comes to games? Here are my suggestions:

- *Alphas*: This can be an internal release in the company, for developers and designers to test and give feedback. Perhaps created for a small set of company fans for larger studios. Friends and family are also good options. It should be small in scale and have a lot of control. It can be classified as a stage of playable prototypes, as they are the ones that present a more complete concept of parts of the game. It is possible to create MVGs from alphas and determine if other game ideas are viable from the selected mechanics.

- *Internal demos*: In large productions, it is common to have demos every year; that is, demonstrations of the games that are being produced for the producer and higher ups, in order to determine the next steps. It is a stage of validation and continuity.

- *Demos*: Who doesn't like to watch a demo being played on the Internet by YouTubers, TikTokers, and Instagrammers? These can be great ways to make your game known to the public and generate engagement, not to mention that all kinds of feedback can be positive for your game. It can be considered an MVG threshold, but in practice it is an MVP, as it checks if the idea is viable and has traction.

- *Betas*: In this case, you can reach a more general public. Take advantage of this step to get feedback, identify flaws, bugs, and missing features, and determine what your game's strengths and weaknesses are. It is definitely a stage to be considered as an MVG, as the game is ready to be played.

- *Soft launches or early launches (prelaunches)*: These are important stages that allow you to assess how much your product is worth. At this stage, as your game should be almost complete, it's a good idea to get as much feedback as possible and fix any missing bugs. If you haven't reached an MVG so far, it's past time, because you already have something you want to profit from, and you're no longer validating whether the idea is viable. The first stage of post-MVG delivery, I would expect that a few iterations past the MVG have already been completed. You could potentially have multiple soft lunches.

- *Marketing launches*: The marketing department is also part of the game team and will use its resources. What about a site that allows those people to play a small feature of the game?

- *Public launches*: In this case, it is desirable that your project be in a position to be released to the general public, well validated, and well tested. This is a value delivery stage after the soft launch, in which the first problems have been identified and corrected. The MVG has been validated and iterated over and new concepts have been validated in past soft launches.

- *Cross-platform launches*: The best option is to launch the game first on a single platform, then expand to others. That doesn't mean it needs to come after the public launch, I personally think it is better, but this could be done as iterations after the soft launch. This is where the game is published on different platforms. Many publishers have recently adopted this model. This is a new value delivery, generally considering that the gameplay is already adequate.

- *Cross-promotion options*: This is yet another stage of strong publicity, which has high added value, as at this stage you can learn what to do better in the next games, by analyzing the feedback received. It's a future learning stage.

- *Updates*: This stage is not mandatory, like any of the previous ones, but it is interesting to know that your game can be improved in its different aspects with the presence of updates. Without the Internet, it was impossible to improve a game; nowadays, updates are quite frequent. With this step, you can start talking about continuous delivery to the customer.

- *Seasons/DLC*: This is a very common engagement technique, which typically includes new content, players, and levels. Sometimes this leads to a whole new short game using the IP (Intellectual Property) and telling a new story.

A nice example of an MVP can be found at Ubisoft's creative process website, where they state that the concept of *Just Dance* came about as a minigame from the game *Raving Rabbids*. The minigame was so loved by

Raving Rabbids players that a group of Ubisoft developers teamed up to create the game's first title. An MVG created from a minigame became a very successful franchise.

Getting More from Less

It's important to always be open to receiving feedback, even checking out ratings and comments on Apple Store, Google Play, Steam, PSN, and Xbox Live. Another good way to measure your success is to use a Twitter account to receive important feedback about the game. In short, be proactive when searching for feedback.

Remember that people are more likely to give you feedback when something is not working right, or not well-tuned, in the game. Try to compare the feedback you get with the initial vision of the game. Try to keep the following in mind regarding MVPs (in this case, MVGs and prototypes):

> *The minimum viable product is that version of a new product that allows the team to collect the maximum learning from clients with minimum effort.*
>
> —Eric Ries (2011), author of *The Lean Startup*

Now, you may be wondering how *minimum* an MVP can be. According to Ries, "Probably much smaller than you think." Does this idea also apply to games? I believe so, especially when you consider the stages described previously. If your game has a feature that can be cut out while the game continues to be viable, it is probably not part of your MVP. In the case of *Super Mario Bros.* (see Figure 4-2), what would the MVP be?

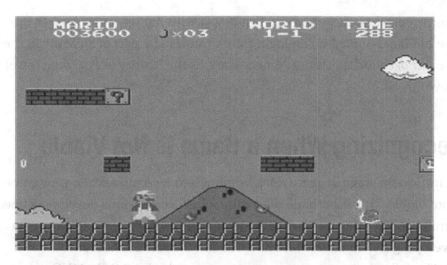

Figure 4-2. *Image of the first version Super Mario Bros. Source:* www.goliath.com/interest/super-mario-bros/

In the minimum viable game of *Super Mario Bros.*, what features are required? It's likely that most people would think about mushrooms, Yoshi, Koopas, pipes, fire flowers, and hidden blocks, but certainly the answer is no to all of those items. The minimum features are "walk," "jump," and maybe "fall in the moat" in a single level. If that's fun and exciting, other features can be added to complement the game experience—and that's what made *Mario* a successful platform game, which developed from a game with a shallow story to a game rich in side stories, contained in a great universe.

You don't believe this could be an MVG? I have a few examples of this in autorun mode: *Canabalt, Jetpack Joyride, Tomb Runner, Temple Run, Subway Surfers,* and *Ski Safari.* Essentially, it's necessary to test the game foundations before adding content because that facilitates feedback about the basics.

What about an RPG like *Final Fantasy*? The *core* of the game would come down to the battle system, which can be similarly seen in many other games, such as *Pokémon Red/Blue.* People played *Pokémon* and *Final Fantasy* to enjoy Pokémon battles and people battles. If the battles were bad, the rest of the game would not be interesting. Therefore, the game does not need quality graphics, just blocks with names and colors. In the case of *Final Fantasy,* an engaging story can also be part of an MVP; in the case of *Pokémon*, this is not so necessary, as the history of *Pokémon* is well known by all.

Recognizing When a Game Is Not Viable

An important stage in game development is to recognize when your game is not viable. This is perhaps one of the toughest decisions developers need to make, but it's necessary many times. No one wants to spend two years developing 2,000 features and find out that the game is not fun.

The following are some ways to measure whether MVPs, MVGs, increments/iterations, and prototypes are interesting:

- *Exploding Kittens*: We all like board games and card games because they allow us to interact with other people, especially when they combine kittens and grenades. Board games are products of high production, from the layout to the game design to the manufacturing. Therefore, it's important to know from the start whether people are going to be interested in the product you are developing. Aside from wanting to get your investment back, you will want some profit as well. A great way of determining whether your idea is worth it is to start a Kickstarter campaign, with videos, blog posts, Twitter, forms, and so on. That will allow you to see whether your idea has flaws.

- *Registration forms*: A good way to start your project is to create a page describing your idea and containing a registration form that allows people to participate on an email list, get updates, offer feedback and make suggestions, and get notifications when the game is launched. Perhaps you could even give these people early access to your game or use the page to measure people's interest in it.

- *Twitter wanderings*: Showing conceptual artwork and ideas of your game design can give other people ideas, but can also allow you to get some great feedback. You can also use Twitter to share other information as well.

- *Cardboard de facto*: This idea doesn't apply to every game, but it works for many. A board game inspired by a software game that is going to be developed can be a good start for setting mechanics, coming up with features, and exploring your creativity. Who knows, maybe it even turns into a real project. But the most important part is to check whether your idea is good and whether it's worth putting into practice.

- *Itch.io*: I particularly like the strategy of releasing small games with some new features and old 3D art/models on platforms like itch.io, as they are more flexible than platforms like Steam. This can help you get feedback, identify improvements to features, or even identify uninteresting features.

- *Game clips and streams*: This is something we see both indie games and AAA games do. In that case, I want to mention the indie games *Veloren* and *BiteMe Games*, which I have started following quite recently. I have personally followed many game developers on YouTube and Twitch that regularly showcase their games.

Thinking Simple First

A good way to start game development is to determine the simplest thing to do in an MVG and then set that as a goal. In my opinion, a great way to start developing games via MVGs is to go through the following list of games and identify each one's MVG. The following list is ordered from the simplest to the hardest in relation to the difficulty of obtaining an MVG, in my opinion:

- Race games: *Need for Speed*

- Top-down shooters (shooting games with the camera orthogonal to the field): *Halo Spartan Assault*

- 2D platform: *Mario*

- Puzzles: *Tetris*

- 3D platform: *Mirror's Edge*

- First-person shooter (FPS): *Call of Duty*

- Japanese RPG (JRPG): *Final Fantasy*

- Fighting games: *Street Fighter*

- Action-adventure: *Tomb Raider*

- RPGs: *Skyrim*

- Real-time strategy (RTS): *Age of Empires*

Multiplayer games have an extra degree of complexity on top of this order.

Tip   Think of MVPs (in this case, MVGs and prototypes) according to Figure 4-3. MVPs must occur incrementally so that each MVP has some return.

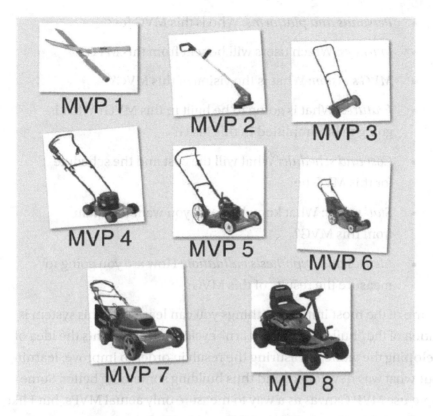

Figure 4-3. *MVP example. Source:* www.caroli.org/produto-viavel-minimo-mvp

From the MVP Canvas to Lean Game Development

The MVP canvas is a model to validate ideas. It was developed in the book *Lean Startup* and is a visual card that describes the elements of an MVP, such as the vision, hypotheses, metrics, features, personas, journeys, and even finances (www.caroli.org/the-mvp-canvas/). So, think of the MVP canvas for game development like this:

- *Personas and platforms*: Who is this MVG for?

- *Journeys*: Which users will benefit from this MVG?

- *MVG's vision*: What is the vision of this MVG?

- *Features*: What is going to be built in this MVG? What is going to be simplified in this MVG?

- *Cost and schedule*: What will the cost and the schedule for this MVG be?

- *Statements*: What knowledge do you want to obtain from this MVG?

- *Metrics and hypothesis validation*: How are you going to measure the results of this MVG?

One of the most important things you can learn with this system is the idea of the "build-measure-learn" cycle. This represents the idea of developing the game, measuring the result in order to improve, learning about what was developed, and thus building something better. Some people use MVP Canvas as a way to measure only actual MVPs, but I like to use it as a way to measure an MVP and its increments, as a game, or a product. Delivery is an incremental process.

In this case, the MVP will be measured, built, and "studied" from a simple model of idealization. When building the MVG and testing it, you can use this line of thought:

> "We believe that the **[MVP vision]** will achieve the **[expected result]**. And, we know this happened based on **[metrics to validate game hypotheses]**."

The following is how my team developed the previous items:

> "We believe in the well-structured fundamental mechanics of the game. We will manage to provide better entertainment than a game full of features.

We know this happened based on the average time
per game per user and in feedback that talks about
the quality of our mechanics."

MVGs and Prototypes of Super Jujuba Sisters

Let's consider the game described in the previous section, which we
named *Super Jujuba Sisters*, and its specifications. One way to determine
the most important features is to have the team put all the features into a
canvas and, later, to collaboratively organize them in order of importance.
To do this, the team can put them into a graphic canvas, in which one
axis corresponds to the priority and the other axis indicates the technical
difficulty in implementing the features.

From that, you can see a logical evolution of MVGs. Figure 4-4 shows
this concept, and Figure 4-5 shows how you can sequence the features to
establish the division of prototypes and MVGs.

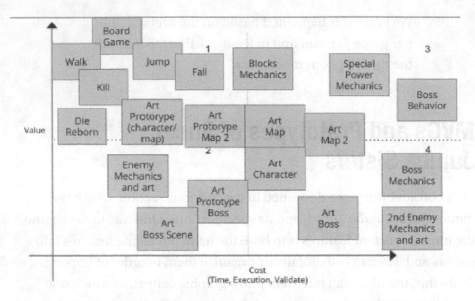

Figure 4-4. *Canvas showing the relationship between priority and technical difficulty*

Sequencer

Board Game	Walk	Jump	Fall	Art Prototype Map and Character	Die and Reborn	Enemy - Mechanic/ Art prototype
Kill	Character Final Art	Special Power	Map 2 Prototype Art	Map Final Art	Block Mechanic	Enemy 2 - Mechanic/ Art Prototype
Moving Blocks Mechanics	Map 2 Final Art	Boss Behavior	Boss Prototype Art	Boss Scene Art	Boss Mechanic	Boss Final Art

Figure 4-5. *Feature sequencer to generate MVPs and MVGs*

Dividing Your MVGs

Here is the evolution of the MVGs:

- Prototype 1
  - Game mechanics to walk, jump, and fall
  - Prototyped layout for the main character and map
- Prototype 2
  - Mechanics to be reborn, killed, and die
  - Mechanics of enemy 1 of the Xandra gang
  - Prototyped layout for enemy 1
  - Layout for the main character
- Prototype 3
  - Mechanics for special power
  - Layout for special power
  - Layout for enemy 1
- Prototype 4
  - Layout for new map
  - Mechanics of hidden blocks
- Prototype 5
  - Mechanics for enemy 2
  - Prototyped layout for enemy 2
- Prototype 6
  - Layout of scenario 3
  - Mechanics of moving blocks

- Prototype 7
  - Mechanics for Marcibal
  - Prototyped layout for Marcibal
- Prototype 8
  - Marcibal's behaviors
  - Marcibal's scenario layout

Splitting the MVGs or Increments

Therefore, we can split the MVGs as follows:

- *MVG0*: Board game to test mechanics and layouts
- *MVG*: Prototype 1 + Prototype 2
- *Increment-1*: MVG + Prototype 3 + Prototype 4
- *Increment-2*: Increment-1 + Prototype 5 + Prototype 6
- *Alfa*: Increment-2 + Prototype 7 + Prototype 8

Summary

In this chapter, you learned what an MVP is and how this concept can be applied to games. You also learned how MVPs are generated and how they can work from the point of view of development and continuous delivery. You learned about MVG metrics and the importance of creating hypotheses to guide you through iterations.

You also learned about the functions and the roles of people engaged in the vision created by MVGs. You saw an example of splitting MVGs for a game, and you learned that you need hypotheses and metrics to measure, analyze, and guide the development process.

CHAPTER 5

MVPs in Practice

This chapter briefly discusses some that have developed games by implemented prototyping, MVGs, and continuous delivery strategies. This is a collection of public articles, post-mortem, documentaries, and talks that they gave about the topic.

Guerrilla Games: From FPS *Killzone* to the Open World of *Horizon Zero Dawn*

Guerrilla Games is the studio responsible for the linear first-person shooter *Killzone* and the open-world, third-person action game *Horizon Zero Dawn,* released in 2017 for PlayStation—a radical change in style. In early 2011, the studio was interested in a new title and opened up the space for everyone in the studio to come up with their own ideas. The initial concept went far beyond the technical knowledge that Guerrilla Games had and the project was considered too risky, causing the studio leadership to pay little attention to the project. Thus, the team started to develop a parallel game similar to *Killzone*, but the idea of *Horizon Zero Dawn* was always present, leading the team to propose the new concept to Sony.

© Julia Naomi Rosenfield Bocira 2024
J. N. Rosenfield Boeira, *Lean Game Development*,
https://doi.org/10.1007/978-1-4842-9843-5_5

Conception Phase

As the studio developed *Killzone: Shadowfall*, a small group (approximately ten people) began to envision *Horizon Zero Dawn,* with the aim of answering important questions such as:

- What would the combat mechanics for fighting the machines, the game enemies?

- What kind of open world would the game have?

- What skills should the player have?

- What would the game's main narrative be?

- How could we make the game playable as soon as possible?

At that point in development, the studio only had the skills and resources to create games like *Killzone*. However, the team's ambition and focus helped them develop the most incredible machine they could think of—the so-called *Thunderjaw*.

Thunderjaw

The idea behind starting development with Thunderjaw was that if they could create a machine interesting enough that had the desired combat mechanics, smaller machines could easily be created from that initial concept. Thus, they started by creating a "Lego" version of what would become Thunderjaw and then virtualized this conception (see Figure 5-1).

Figure 5-1. *Virtualized Lego version of Thunderjaw*

Interestingly, many of the concepts created for *Thunderjaw* made it into the final game. Figure 5-1 shows how the "Lego" version of Thunderjaw looked, while Figure 5-2 shows what each Lego part represented.

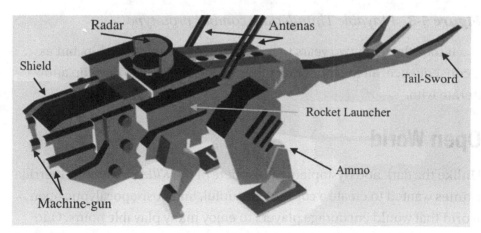

Figure 5-2. *Thunderjaw parts*

In the initial Thunderjaw combat mechanics prototype, you can see all these parts and that the main character is a *Killzone* character with a *Killzone* weapon—that is, because the idea was to test the mechanics of Thunderjaw, which meant making the simplest prototype possible. This is shown in Figure 5-3.

Figure 5-3. *Playable Thunderjaw combat prototype*

It took the team two years to have Thunderjaw ready to ship, but as a consequence, all the other machines were quite easy to develop and iterate with.

Open World

Unlike the dark and dystopian atmosphere of the *Killzone* games, Guerrilla Games wanted to create a colorful, beautiful, and post-apocalyptic open world that would encourage players to enjoy many playable hours. One of the bases for modeling the different scenarios was watching hundreds of hours of nature documentaries, focusing on animal behavior and landscapes. The first focus of the open world ended up changing due to the complexity of nature and the team decided to create a city, as they already had the necessary knowledge due to *Killzone*. The initial city, Meridian, was conceived as a central part of the game and ended up being carried into final production, even though it was almost irrelevant and much smaller than the initial concept.

Figure 5-4. *Meridian prototype*

Figure 5-4 shows that the initial prototype to walk around Meridian contained an ordinary horse, but they decided to change that to a machine-horse, as they believed that a normal horse would look strange in a world full of machine-animals. In addition, the horse needed to explore a giant, open world. Considering the horse would move around in a large, open world, two gameplay concepts were created using it, as shown in Figures 5-5 and 5-6.

Figure 5-5. *Walking around a florist with the horse*

Figure 5-6. *Hunting with the horse*

Note that in these two figures, the horse is not a machine, but as the goal was to create mechanics and gameplay, there was no problem using a non-machine horse. These two features resulted in a third system that managed the path-finding for the horse, so that it could avoid colliding with other game objects. As some of those game objects were constantly moving, the path-finding feature needed to adapt quickly to changes in game objects positions. This new system is shown in Figure 5-7.

Figure 5-7. Horse path-finding system

Vegetation Navigation

One of the main features of the game is the ability to hide in the vegetation to avoid attracting the attention of the machines. Thus, a new prototype was created to verify silent and non-silent navigation in vegetation (see Figure 5-8). In addition, in the initial concept, *Horizon* was going to be a local cooperative multiplayer game. This was given up due to the fact that a local multiplayer in an open world would require sacrificing vegetation and machine details.

Figure 5-8. *Silent coop vegetation navigation*

Finally, the Proof of Concept

It was 2014 and time to create a proof of concept to demonstrate the game's potential. With that, all prototypes were brought together in a single playable, with the new art and mechanics integrated. It was almost like an MVG.

Figure 5-9. *Proof of concept screenshot*

Note how close the proof of concept shown in Figure 5-9 is to the actual playable game. However, this proof of concept generated many questions:

- What is the size and density that an open world should have?

- What variety of character skills would there be and how would they be unlocked?

- What would the game narrative be?

These questions led to the final map size being one-fifth the size of the initial map size, because they concluded that the map would need to be much smaller to keep an interesting density so that the game would maintain player engagement.

Preproduction

After the release of *Killzone: Shadowfall* and a very successful proof of concept, Guerrilla Games was able to allocate enough people to the development of this game, growing the team from approximately 10 to 180 people. The focus was on creating journeys, activities, characters, and machines, and defining the story. During the conception phase, 20 different stories were created to explore all the elements of the prototypes and how they related. It was necessary to create a single unified story, but the team had very little experience in this, since the *Killzone* story was usually done by third parties. Thus, the playable demo was ready in 2016 and it was a great success, which greatly increased the anticipation about the game and proved that the MVG was successful.

Production

The main issue that the team noticed in the production phase was the relevance of combat with humans, as machines did not speak. It was necessary to make the story more engaging and this made combat against humans go from something secondary to a relevant part of the game, along with combat against machines. Data collected in the MVG was used as a basis for game balancing, due to its complexity.

Finally, in 2017, *Horizon Zero Dawn* was released. In a subsequent stage of production, at the end of the same year, there was the release of an expansion, *The Frozen Wilds*. In 2022, the sequel, *Horizon Forbidden West,* was released. This was certainly Guerrilla Games' most famous and successful IP.

To learn more about the *Horizon Zero Dawn* development process, you can check out the following videos:

- The Making of *Horizon Zero Dawn,* by Noclip (2017), available at `www.youtube.com/watch?v=h9tLcD1r-6w`

- *Horizon Zero Dawn*: *A Game Design Postmortem,* by GDC (2018), available at `www.youtube.com/watch?v=TawhcWao9ls`

Archero

A great example of games that use MVP are hypercasual and free-to-play (F2P) games. These games start with a small MVP idea to see if there's engagement in the concept and then evolve based on the users' needs. One of the main examples of this segment and, possibly, a game that defined this strategy in the mobile market is *Archero*, by Habby/Monduz Games.

The Habby studio team for this game was composed of 12 very experienced hypercasual games developers, people who had worked on games such as *Piano Tiles,* from Cheetah Games. Given this background, the team was aware of what it would take to focus on this market segment. Thus, *Archero* was a game that brought a number of interesting learnings to the hypercasual and F2P gaming industries:

- *Archero* demonstrated that it is possible to create a hypercasual and F2P game inspired by other segments, such as the indie segment, which tends to be more creative. The game is basically an Arcade RPG compressed for mobile. How did they manage to create a successful Arcade RPG in a segment that is not used to it? They focused on the mechanics they believed were most relevant to the hypercasual RPG experience. The lesson *is not to limit yourself to the game models that your segment presents.*

- They validated the game idea through targeted marketing, hypercasual gamers, and/or RPG players and did this by focusing their videos and campaigns in an art direction that was pleasing in these markets.

- UX, the user experience, which is the key to any game. In the case of *Archero,* the learning comes from the fact that *the UX of the game focuses on the simplicity of the core loop,* with recurring feedbacks of what is happening in the screen and mechanics that have evolved to make the game extremely attractive.

- Another key point of this game's UX is the *simplicity of learning the mechanics and the wonderful experience of playing the game the first time,* unlocking new mechanics throughout the player's evolution, as game metrics are collected to create new mechanics.

Dead Cells

Dead Cells is a game worth highlighting for the creative and collaborative process of Motion-Twin, its developer. Motion-Twin's marketing specialist stated that the team's mindset for developing this game was this:

> "Let's make a game that we'd like to play. A very *hardcore*, super niche, pixel art, and extremely difficult game. Let's make our passion as a project and not care about the consequences."

It is worth mentioning that Motion-Twin started as a game development cooperative, in which all members received the same salary and there was no traditional hierarchical system. This enables a creative process in which all parties have the same value when exposing ideas, which also allows for a healthy work style and a good balance between personal and work life. One of the downsides of this process is that decisions can be time consuming.

The Foundation for Dead Cells

Dead Cells is a game that had many learnings from the creation process of the game *Hordes Zero* (and *Die2Nite*, a browser game prequel to *Hordes Zero*). During the beta testing phase of the first *Hordes Zero* concept, the game proved difficult to engage and unattractive in single player mode. This made it difficult for players to engage until reaching multiplayer mode, which would happen later. Due to the single player engaging problems, the game was converted into a simple 2D tower defense rather than an exploratory game with occasional tower defense. At the same time, Motion-Twin constantly published their art and concepts for the game and, with the conversion to a simple 2D tower defense, it was possible to detect that the arts for the first game concept no longer made sense for the current state of the project, so a new concept was launched.

This allowed for a nice MVP for *Hordes Zero,* which consisted of a cooperative multiplayer tower defense game that would eventually become competitive.

Finally, the opportunity to test the MVP and receive feedback would happen at Gamescom; however, it is difficult to test a multiplayer game at a gaming conference, which made MVP for the conference a single player game where all multiplayer entities are controlled by the user, making it easier to demo the game at events like that. Two of the main lessons learned from Gamescom were 1) few people could easily pronounce the name of the game, *Hordes Zero,* and 2) users found the new single player mode was very interesting. Thus, the game's new name became *Dead Cells,* as the game was no longer consistent with the idea of a sequel to *Die2nite,* in relation to both art and concept.

Dead Cells Multiplayer

For a period of three months, the new *Dead Cells* entered the alpha testing phase as a multiplayer game for, initially, 30 players. Feedback for the multiplayer mode remained the same: "the game was interesting only when all participants were online at the same time." Due to the uncertainty about the game's future and the feedback from the community about the multiplayer mode, Motion-Twin had to put the project on hold to get more funding and, inevitably, the game stopped for almost a year. The objective was to have the game on hold until funds were raised, so that the team could better plan the game's future and the team could focus on finishing existing projects.

After that, there was another setback in the development of *Dead Cells:* the project's technical leaders no longer wanted to develop mobile games, but more "hardcore" PC games. This motivated the entire team to stop developing mobile games, as they realized that it was a very competitive market, which would require more investment and time. This change also caused the team to change the core features of the game, which became single player mode, ceased to be free-to-play, and no longer a tower defense. At this point, it was a completely new game from the initial plan. In addition, there was one more restriction for the game: the studio had funds to develop the game for only 12 months.

Abandoning the Tower Defense

With the new focus, the MVP presented at Gamescom was no longer aligned with the team goals and a new MVP would need to be built to test the game's hypotheses in a new market. Fortunately, the learnings from *Hordes Zero* and *Dead Cells* multiplayer were still valuable. The entire tower defense mechanic was replaced with a permanent death mechanic, which followed a *kill, die, learn, and repeat* model. This model starts each cycle from scratch, but allows new paths and explorations of the scenario, learning the behaviors of the NPCs, just like in the famous *Castlevania*.

Another important learning was captured from another game, *No Man's Sky,* in which the procedural generation of terrain and massive levels proved traumatizing and meaningless for players. Thus, the dungeon generation system focused on short and simple generations, enabling new experiences each time the game was played. Unfortunately, this caused a feeling of lack of permanence, which generated discomfort in the players.

Fortunately, games like *Spelunky, Faster Than Light,* and *Left 4 Dead* had already solved this problem. The team focused on learning how these other games had developed those types of randomized scenarios. With this, the team was able to set a value of 50 percent procedural, based on player development, and 50 percent predefined, changing the game to a platformer. To make it easier for players to onboard on a strange, vibrant, and partly procedural map, a color system across settings and NPCs made it easy to identify the iteration with each region or character.

The New MVP

One of the main points of the MVP was to deal with character arts, scenarios, and their animations—all done by just one artist. The conclusion was to use base 3D models to generate animations and facilitate the reuse of weapons, armor, and animations. After all this time, funding for the game was running low and the studio decided to release the game as early access on Steam to secure funds to finish the game. Thus, early access needed to survive the *indiepocalypse*, which is the fact that many games from indie studios are slaughtered upon release because they do not contain a core mechanic and, in the case of early access, they lack a vertical slice of what the game will be.

The prototype released in early access ensured great constructive feedback and positive reviews, indicating that the game was going the right way, which showed the team that the game was valid and indicated which areas of the game needed improvements. Furthermore, constructive feedback forged, possibly, 50 percent of the game's new mechanics and concepts. When the game was finally released, expert reviews called the game "early access done right." Subsequently, a series of DLCs (downloadable content) was created for *Dead Cells* and a series of free updates were made.

Notes on the Game Design Document for MVP

For non-game designers like myself, the game design document (GDD) usually means a giant document that very few people will care about. However, that is far from what it is and doesn't describe the creative process behind it. Games usually have to start somewhere, and that somewhere is usually a character, a mechanistic idea, or a concept. However, translating a concept to a game is a pretty heavy task. With that said, let me recap the aspects of the process I see as beneficial from the Lean perspective.

A game usually starts with a passion, a market demand, an idea, or a concept in the back of someone's mind. This is a nice first step, but that is still far from an end goal. Design is a creative process and most design disciplines praise collaborative work and lots and lots of feedback. So a creative and collaborative process needs to start somewhere. My suggestion is having a *box cover*[1] of your idea and discuss it with the team to collect feedback.

Once the team agrees with the idea, present the box cover in the kick-off meeting of a Lean inception to give direction and help foster ideas during the brainstorm phase. After the inception, the team will have a bunch of unstructured ideas based on the box cover and a possible MVP with its iterations. Take this next phase as an MVP consolidation phase. Its goal is to capture the whole inception as a one-page design document that the team uses to start working on the game and that the concept artists use to create ideas about the concept.

Once the development has started, especially after a few iterations, there will be a need for a denser game design document (GDD). This ten-page design document is where you can easily add information based on the development process and feedback while continuing to define where the game should be. To me, the ten-page design document is something that should be the next stage of the MVP. This doesn't mean that you should not work on the design document from one page to ten pages, but you need to keep it open enough so that the feedback and validations from MVP can easily be added.

Once your MVP is validated, the design team will need to start working on making this ten-page design document a complete game design document that can serve as a reference to development. However, this is the moment I usually notice that the project starts to drift away, as some

---

[1] A simple design document that consists of adding your ideas for the game as a game box cover, where you describe it with a concept name, a concept art, two or three features, images, and key bullet points.

designers are eager to reinvent the wheel after the MVP has been validated and add non-validated ideas to the project as written in stone rules. This introduced bugs and things that can possibly break the game design in large teams.

> *"The design document should be the foundations, the core skeleton, the knowns, and the guiding lights. Add layers as you validate or have good inspiration to test, explore, and get feedback, but avoid long, extensive, exhaustive, speculative, fluff out of the doc, as it will likely lead to fewer people being able to actually absorb any of it. Design docs should be very focused, prefer "living" (functional gameplay sections that highlight important pieces) design docs where possible. If pictures are worth 1,000 words, a functional, representative section of gameplay is worth a million words."*

—Evan Boehler

The learning I want game developers to take from this is to actively participate, give feedback, and own the development process from the design perspective. While, specifically for game designers, I recommend not adding features, mechanics, and ideas without having them tested somehow, especially within the whole game concept. As you have seen in this chapter, many ideas work perfectly alone, but do not merge well with other ideas. For more information, I recommend Scott Rogers' *Level Up* book.

Summary

In this chapter, you learned how several game productions used Lean concepts to develop their games and how the GDD relates to that process:

- From *Horizon*, you learned about prototyping, testing, and evolving ideas.

- From *Archero*, you learned how the hypercasual and free-to-play games develop their projects in a way that is increasingly engaging.

- From *Dead Cells*, you learned about the feedback process and how to define MVPs.

CHAPTER 6

Generating Hypotheses

Along with the creation of minimum viable games (MVGs), hypotheses are one of the most important parts of an inception because they guide and measure your product through iterations. The MVGs determine which set of activities must be done, while hypotheses allow you to validate if your MVGs have the desired effect and if the product's vision is being met.

The first generation of hypotheses is intuitive because it's part of the inception, which is the initial stage of development. But what is the role of hypotheses? Their first function is to help develop the game design, help build the narrative, and (most important) help validate the MVG.

However, the main difference between hypotheses and stories is that stories guide the development, while hypotheses continuously feed the backlog. Let's use the examples of stories generated at the example inception to generate hypotheses.

Remember the personas presented in Chapter 3? There are two cases in which you want to use them as guides to generate hypotheses. The journeys of personas and the stories developed are as follows:

- Like Guilherme, I want the game to remind me of old video game times; therefore, I want an experience like *Mario* 2.0.

© Julia Naomi Rosenfield Boeira 2024
J. N. Rosenfield Boeira, *Lean Game Development*,
https://doi.org/10.1007/978-1-4842-9843-5_6

- Like Carlita, I want to be able to make the "princess" save the day; therefore, I want the main character to be a woman.

- Like Guilherme, it's important to jump, walk, and fall.

- Carlita wants Jujuba to be a strong character and, just like in *Frozen* (the Disney animated film), wants things to revolve around the sisters.

Based on these stories and journeys, you could come to the following hypotheses:

- We believe that building the features of walking, jumping, and falling into the game will result in a game with strong basic mechanics. We know we've been successful when we have positive feedback from third-parties through our demo and manual testing.

- We believe that by building a strong non-stereotypical female character, with interesting functionalities, we will be able to reach the female audience, who will be excited by our game. We know that we have been successful when lots of girls start to comment in our feed.

The standard model for developing hypotheses during inceptions is as follows (GOTHELF, 2013):

We believe that by building the feature **[name of the feature]** for the audience **[intended audience]**, we'll achieve **[expected outcomes]**.

We will know that we were successful when we have **[the expected market signal]**.

When Hypotheses Are Not Created from the Inception

Hypotheses help you validate things in every cycle. They are fundamental to completing the measurement and analysis steps because they set the validations you have to make. For instance, if you get negative feedback from the female audience regarding the main character, you should stop and analyze where you are and start developing new ideas using that feedback.

Here are some examples of possible measures:

- When you realize the female audience is offended by the character, you have to read the criticisms (for example, is it the clothes, nonexistent armor, disproportionate body, nonsensical story, or lack of story?), check what you did wrong, and think of new solutions to generate hypotheses. This doesn't mean that the character is not engaging or valid. It could mean that the criticism is about how the character is portrayed.

- When you realize the audience has complained that the jump mechanics are visually ugly and give the impression that the character is moving abruptly upward and downward, you have to consider the problem. Is it an issue of improving the animation? Is it that it doesn't look real? Is it not adequate to the game's needs? At this point, it's necessary to determine which stage you went wrong and suggest new modeling.

- If you realize that the audience complained that the first level is pretty cool but the other ones are exactly the same, making the game uninteresting, how can you make the other levels more appealing? Can you add new characters? Is the game mood poorly conceived? Are there proper obstacles in the scenario? It's necessary to determine what is missing and come up with new ideas to make the user experience more interesting. The inverse is also important to consider— is the first level too packed with all the best mechanics? Should you pace them out? Should the first level be moved to a later stage of the game?

These examples show the need to elaborate on the hypotheses to ensure you reach your goals. Just keep in mind that all feedback is valuable, but not all feedback is valid, and not all feedback is articulated enough to identify an issue. Feedback helps you get another perspective on your work and generate new insights. Chapter 10 talks more about feedback.

Summary

In this chapter, you saw how to extract hypotheses from stories, journeys, and personas, as well as how hypotheses are great sources of support for MVGs. You also learned how to generate ideas and how they work in a cycle of many iterations.

Now you need to understand things from a more practical and less theoretical point of view so that you have the resources to guide you in the next steps of Lean development, such as test-driven development and continuous integration. These topics are discussed in the next chapter.

CHAPTER 7

Test-Driven Development

TDD (test-driven development) is a style of software development presented mainly by Kent Beck's Extreme Programming (XP) Agile method. The practice involves the implementation of a system from the test cases of an object. In this chapter, you learn how TDD can be applied to games from the theoretical perspective and which practices can improve your development experience when developing with TDD.

When writing test cases, the code is implemented based on the demand of each test. You must write a test and, soon after, implement your solution to that test, avoiding writing several tests and codes at the same time. Thus, you'll have a continuous cycle of small iterations.

Although the literature on this subject is extensive and qualified, it is worth including this chapter to delve into the topics presented, since it is a subject of extreme importance, especially because it is not common to find game developers who have experience developing games with TDD.

© Julia Naomi Rosenfield Boeira 2024
J. N. Rosenfield Boeira, *Lean Game Development*,
https://doi.org/10.1007/978-1-4842-9843-5_7

TDD Defined

TDD is a software development style in which you have the following at your disposal:

- An enormous set of tests created by the people who wrote the code (no code in production without a test and without it having been tested).

- A method in which the test is written first.

- Code written so that its only goal is to pass the test in a simple way.

- Code with less redundancy and more elegance.

- More extensible code.

The code developer writes the tests, determining in advance which tests are necessary and how they should be ordered to implement the code. The code is written after the tests and conceived only to pass the previously written test. One of the advantages of this method is that it implies "thinking before developing." Of course, a test expert can be consulted.

The following are additional important aspects of TDD:

- *Run the code often*: TDD allows you to get a visual of the code's general status.

- *Maintain the whole code tested in the smallest units*: The simpler and more unitary the code, the easier it is to fix build issues and tests that fail.

- *Treat tests that fail as broken builds*: All tests should pass every time before continuing.

- *Keep testing simple*: Complex tests may not be testing the desired unit or acting as unitary tests (TDD can involve many other test types than unit tests).

- *Tests should be independent from each other*: Each test should be testing isolated units, features, or components.

Here are some advantages of TDD:

- The software becomes more understandable and easier to implement.

- Allows for simpler solutions.

- Results in fewer defects.

In fact, TDD can make your code more elegant. Furthermore, it can work pretty well as a form of documentation. I should emphasize that people often confuse the two TDD concepts of unit testing and test first. To simplify, TDD ➤ Test First[1] ➤ Only Unit Testing ➤ Only Integration Testing[2].

In other words, TDD combines a test-first strategy, unit/integration testing, and continuous refactors to design the coding workflow. However, the use of unit tests in your code does not necessarily make your development test-driven, because the presence of tests is just part of TDD. As a result, TDD makes the code development and testing process safer, more Agile, and of better quality. Figure 7-1 shows a typical TDD cycle.

---

[1] *Test first*: Testing strategy based on the partial practice of TDD, in which tests are written before implementing the code, but there is not necessarily a refactoring or cyclical process of TDD. This process can lead to more coupled and less elegant code than TDD, containing a lot of redundancy, but with the test cases covered.

[2] *Only unit/integration testing*: Many teams write unit and integration tests for code that has been added. This strategy can lead to tests that don't adequately cover all scenarios, or to tests that only test what the already written code expects. "Been there."

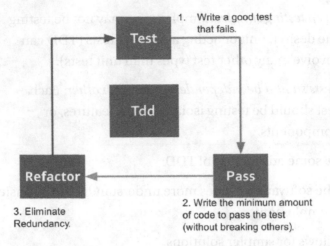

Figure 7-1. *TDD cycle*

As you can see in Figure 7-1, TDD occurs as follows:

1. *Write the test*: Without a test, you don't know where to begin.

2. *Run the test and see it fail*: What's the use of a test if you know it's going to pass? It has to fail.

3. *Write the code*: It's time to write the minimum code for that test to pass (without breaking other tests).

4. *Run the test and see it pass*: "Wow! Now it passed!" Your code is correct.

5. *Refactor*: Certainly there are things that can be improved in the code.

6. *Iterate*: Go on to the next test.

Tests Are Good, So Why Is There So Much Poorly Tested Code?

I believe that most companies, in almost every sector, consider tests as something positive. No one wants to wear a bulletproof vest with some material that has never been tested, just like no one wants a software application that was never tested. So why is there so much poorly tested software out there?

It's because the traditional approach to testing has several problems, explained here:

- If the tests are not comprehensive enough, errors can end up in production, causing devastating effects.

- Tests are usually created after the code is written. When you have already completed your programming activity, coming back to an earlier version of the software can be irksome.

- Usually, tests are written by developers other than those who wrote the code. As they cannot comprehend the code in its entirety, comprehension and approach errors can happen while writing the tests.

- If the person who writes the test does it based on documentation or other artifacts in addition to the code, any artifact update can make the test obsolete.

- If tests are not automated, they are not going to be executed often, regularly, or in exactly the same way.

- Fixing a problem in a given place can create a problem elsewhere. In this case, if the structure of tests is not comprehensive, it won't detect this new problem.

TDD solves all the following problems:

- The programmer writes the test before the code is written. In this case, the code is based on tests, ensuring testability, comprehensiveness, and synchrony between the test and the code.

- The tests are automated and run frequently.

- When a bug is found, the process allows it to be quickly repaired; this procedure is guaranteed by the test's comprehensiveness.

- When the code is delivered, the tests are also delivered, making it easy to make future changes and extensions in a simple way.

Applying TDD to Games

Game companies usually don't believe that TDD is possible—and this is a mindset shared by their developers. Of course, there are great differences between corporate software and game software, but best practices, tests, and everything else in the Lean methodology can be applied to games indeed.

As an example of this anti-Agile mindset, consider these comments from Rob Galanakis, from his 2014 article "Agile Game Development Is Hard":

- *"Games are art and art cannot be iterated on like other software."* I know the game industry prefers to compare itself to the movie industry rather than the software industry, and I agree that games are art, but art also can be done in small steps (see Figure 7-2).

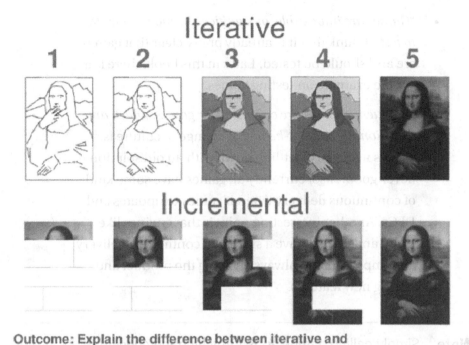

Figure 7-2. Agile methods applied to art. Source: Jeff Patton (http://jpattonassociates.com/dont_know_what_i_want)

- *"Games require too much 'infrastructure' to make anything playable."* Playable for a final user, maybe. But remember that not every delivery needs to be for an end user and be completely feature complete. Feedback midway is important to guide development.

- *"Games want users to spend time, not save time."* Here, the goal is to help the development team save time; the game itself does not have much impact here. Another important point is to make the player learn the mechanics of the game as quickly as possible (a nice lesson learned from hypercasual games), that is, to save the player from unnecessary frustration and allow for greater fun.

85

- *"Games are impossible, or significantly more difficult, to test."* I think that it is already pretty clear that games are and should be tested. Later in this book, there is a simple example on testing games.

- *"Frequent releases are confusing for games, which are traditionally content-heavy."* A change of culture is always necessary; settling down with an old solution is never good. Also, currently all games have some kind of continuous delivery when it comes to updates and DLCs. Another interesting point is that engines like Unity and Unreal have a system of continuous delivery and improvement, always evolving the product and testing new features.

Note   Simply calling games art is stretching the concept of art. I believe that the correct concept that Rob Galanakis wanted to develop is the concept of technical design or even user experience, since game art is a marketing concept that aims to please the audience, and not a manifestation of the author. On the other hand, we do have games that try to be a manifestation of the author's intent.

Later, you'll read about some ways to apply tests to games. Now, I think it is important to present some viable ways to apply TDD:

- Frameworks such as Pygame (`www.pygame.org/`) and MonoGame (`www.monogame.net/`) are great solutions for using tests, especially because they are always being integrated into new versions of programming languages. Furthermore, every game is made via code, which eliminates the difficulty of testing components. However, it increases difficulty from the artistic perspective.

- Unity was one of the first big engines to develop an asset for testing. Previously, this asset was called Unity Test Tools and needed to be added to the engine. Currently, Unity Test Runner is integrated into the engine and is very easy to use, containing many examples and extensive documentation.

- Unreal is an open source C++ engine. With a little dedication from the game development team, it is possible to integrate test libraries. Currently, it has a test plug-in that is mainly focused on functional testing, but supports other levels of testing.

- CryEngine has recently shown interest in enabling integration with its engine. Crytek has provided a lecture called AAA Automated Testing... for AAA games.

- The Bevy engine (my favorite) is a Rust engine that uses ECS and allows you to perform tests in a very simple, controlled, and direct way.

- Using other engines, the solution can be relatively simple. Create a scene that will contain several tests. With empty prefabs or game objects, start to create test conditions. From a test script that you developed, attach the scene and test the specific behavior of your prefabs and scripts.

Note   Prefabs are components premade by the developer that can be reused in other parts of the game. Examples of prefabs are scenery objects, enemies, instantiatable players, and so on.

Here are some examples of tests on Unity:

- *Unity Test Tools: Test automation in Unity now and in the future, Unite Boston 2015*: `https://youtu.be/wJGUc-EeKyw`

- *Unity Test Tools: Test automation in Unity now and in the future, Unite Europe 2015*: `https://youtu.be/_OYojVTaqxY`

Remember, games usually have complex code and many components beyond code. Therefore, it's important to have in mind the simplest test that you can run and figure out how to make it pass in the simplest way possible.

Note   I have faced desperate situations while having to test components from a visual point of view, but the solution was pretty simple: I created a scene that ran automatically, and all components within it started as empty. This scene had a single script to manage tests. As each test was written, the components evolved to the point where I managed to create simple prefabs that were ideal for the applications I needed.

Overcoming the Hurdles

Incorporating TDD into games presents challenges that most software doesn't have, such as the vast number of platforms (Mac, Windows, Linux, Xbox, Nintendo, PlayStation, Switch, iOS, and Android). Thus, you need to run unit tests on each platform that you want your game to run on. Usually, you will keep several builds and check whether they break the tests and in which specific cases this happens.

Another challenge is how to test graphics. It's a best practice in software engineering to keep all the graphic-related code in a single module, which contributes to facilitating tests from other modules. Using engines can make TDD unfeasible since the biggest ones are not TDD friendly—although some of them, such as Unity and Cry, have started to address that.

Randomness is something imperative in games. For instance, it's impossible to predict which walking sound should be played; in addition, running tests for random things is complex. One of the ways to solve randomness when testing is to try to get the most out of the tests that are being tested. Perhaps you can pass it as an argument? There's a clear relation between running tests and reducing bugs.

Making TDD Better

TDD was developed to be used with a series of practices that add value to development. Next, you'll learn about some of them.

Refactoring

Refactoring is the process of making changes in existent and working code, without changing its external behavior. In other words, changing how the code works but not what it does. The goal is to improve the code's internal structure, making it more readable with better performance. For example, after making the code simpler so the test passes, you can refactor it to clean it, especially reducing duplications and potential pattern or style errors.

Or, you make sure refactoring does not break the tests.

Here are times to refactor:

- When there's duplicated code.

- When you realize the code is not clear or readable.

- When you detect potentially dangerous code.

- When there is a pattern or style error that makes the code difficult to use or increases complexity without a reason for it.

Here are some examples of important types of refactoring:

- *Extracting classes/structs/records*: When a structure is too large or its behavior is no longer clear, it is worth splitting it into two or more, so that similar behaviors stay together. Detaching and repurposing blocks of data can also solve simple memory allocation problems.

- *Higher order functions*: When we talk about functional programming, it is common to find duplicate codes in functions that could be simplified by passing a different function block as an argument to the function you want to use.

- *Extracting interfaces/traits/protocols*: You can use refactoring to facilitate using mocks because they represent a group behavior. Furthermore, they allow different structures to behave in the same and expected way in different contexts.

- *Extracting methods/functions*: Refactoring applies when a method is too long or has complex logic. It facilitates understanding methods.

- *Introducing self-explaining variables*: When you need variables that are not clear regarding their function and why they're there, it's good to extract them for a constant that explains its function.

- *Trying to identify patterns*: All repeating patterns can possibly be simplified into a single code block that is used in different contexts.

Pair Programming

Pair programming is not directly included as a practice of TDD, but as a good evangelist of the practice, I believe that both are part of the same set of programming practices. Thus, I believe that pair programming improves team performance with the application of TDD. Some of the benefits of pair programming include the following:

- *Increasing the concentration of developers*: It improves communication among all parties, especially facilitating the identification and resolutions of gaps, in addition to stimulating creative discussion.

- *Reducing defects*: It helps make the code simpler and the reviews more efficient.

- *Keeping business continuity*: The increase of communication reduces the impact if a project member leaves. However, you might face some challenges regarding pair programming, such as work infrastructure, since assembling teams can be complicated, especially in small companies. Furthermore, if your team doesn't have identical configurations for everyone, such as IDEs and editors, it could be hard to implement pair programming. Also, it's necessary to take into account fatigue because it's common to find people exhausted after hours of pair programming.

- *Reducing issues related to ego conflicts*: Perhaps one of the greatest difficulties of many pairings is the lack of communication and humility when arguing. Constructive discussions turn into aggressive arguments, which can be fatal to pair programming.

As everything is done as a pair, it's important to recognize the work done as a pair and not claim individuality over the work. Also, allow space for both people to communicate their ideas and don't gaslight their thoughts. Another thing that can be beneficial for pairing is giving feedback to each other after the session.

Here are some tips for pair programming proposed by Tarso Aires (2015):

- *Don't centralize the driving*: The member of the pair who feels more comfortable in the development environment tends to centralize the driving. It's good to define beforehand an amount of time that each person is in the driver's seat.

- *Manage the focus together*: Having different focuses is extremely common. If this becomes a problem, the more focused partner must bring focus to the less focused one. It can be complicated for the less focused partner to get back their focus alone. Techniques like *pomodoro* should help—it consists of taking little breaks for relaxing.

- *Avoid working alone*: Sometimes one of the individuals of the pair may have to be absent for a while; in this case, it's better to wait for them to get back. Seize the opportunity to do stuff not related to work.

- *Try to mix concentration and relaxation moments*: Focus is essential, but an excess amount of it can be harmful. Remember that we are not robots and we need to rest. Play video games, have a coffee and a conversation, or even take a 15-minute nap.

- *Celebrate the achievements*: At the end of each stage or activity, it's gratifying and empowering to stop and contemplate what was done. Celebrate!

- *Achieve balance*: It's natural that one person will have more experience with the activity. This can bring a difference in the rhythm in which things are being done, harming the pairing. Notice these differences, adapt to your colleague's rhythm, and explain your ideas however many times you find necessary. Communication is essential.

- *Convey the context properly*: It's important to guarantee that both pair members have a common vocabulary. If necessary, draw diagrams and always try to explain as simply and directly as possible.

- *Know how to handle divergences*: Disagreements happen all the time during pairing. In these moments, it's important to stop and listen to everything the other person has to say, answering calmly and respectfully. If necessary, call a third person to help in solving the deadlock.

- *Get ready to learn and to teach*: Keep in mind that you can contribute even if you're new in the project, the same way you can learn new things. Present concepts gradually and guide your partner to the solution subtly and clearly. Listen carefully to whatever is being taught.

- *Exchange feedback*: The pair should have a conversation and exchange feedback while memories are fresh. This could be a 15- to 30-minute conversation or exchanging notes in the proper place.

The most common example in pair programming is two people sharing peripherals and a CPU monitor and working together. Another common way is to use a tool such as Screenhero, which allows the remote person to edit and change the development environment through screen sharing.

Note   If you want to learn more about TDD, check out Chapters 15 and 16.

Summary

In this chapter, you learned about the stages of test-driven development and techniques to improve a team's performance, such as pair programming.

Unfortunately, well-tested code does not always ensure full quality; for example, if the code is not in its latest version, tests might be broken, or the build of the game might not be functioning. This is when you can introduce continuous integration, covered in the next chapter.

CHAPTER 8

Continuous Integration

In this chapter, you learn about the advantages of continuous integration (CI), read about its key concepts, and learn how to apply it to a project. You also learn what continuous integration means for a team. Last, you learn which tools and frameworks are available for implementing continuous integration during game development.

Why Continuous Integration?

The main goal of continuous integration is to find bugs as early as possible and this is done every time the code is modified. In general lines, CI is a set of automated tasks performed when the code is integrated to ensure consistency and quality. Simply put, it goes through the following steps:

- *Bug tracker*: You use a tool to identify bugs.

- *Source control*: You commit the code using some code versioning tool. This tool allows you to verify the current state of the code and all the changes it has gone through. You can use it in association with a build agent. Git and Perforce are the most common in game development.

J. N. Rosenfield Boeira, *Lean Game Development*,
https://doi.org/10.1007/978-1-4842-9843-5_8

- *Build agent*: This is a tool that generates the code's build. Usually, it is a set of commands in an environment, such as Jenkins, GitHub Actions, or CircleCI, with the goal of making builds available automatically.

- *Unit/integration tests*: These tests ensure the added code is compatible with the rest of the project. I believe that mutation tests, which introduce small errors and variations into the code in order to determine the scope of the tests, can help a lot in validating that the tests themselves are useful and that they have a good coverage.

- *Automated functionality tests*: Use this kind of test to check whether all the functions and features are working correctly and whether any are defective.

- *Deploy*: You release a build for use, updates, and manual tests, among other reasons.

Ideally, the integration should take place at least daily, or better, each new test with the corresponding implementation. Every code integration is verified by an automatic build, which makes it easy to spot problems. Furthermore, the practice helps to quickly identify where the error is and prevent defective code from being placed into production.

"Continuous integration doesn't get rid of bugs, but it does make them dramatically easier to find and remove." —Martin Fowler

---

If integration occurs frequently, looking for bugs becomes a simpler job, and the developers will have more time to develop new features. In addition, CI allows the team members to have more clarity regarding the development time since they can spend less time fixing bugs.

These are some of the advantages of continuous integration:

- There won't be any complex and long integrations since the code is integrated every time and each increment is small.

- It increases the visibility of each stage, allowing for better communication. Everyone can follow how their colleagues are developing and in which stage of development they are.

- It facilitates problem identification, allowing you to solve problems immediately. Any problem will be identified as soon as the code runs the automated build. Less time will be spent on debugging and more with features since errors will be quickly identified, without long hours for investigation.

- Trust increases when building a game with a solid foundation, because the tests and the continuous integration will ensure that the errors are small and quickly identified.

- It reduces tension and the mystery of waiting to see whether the code works. Although builds take time, the time to fix them is dramatically reduced.

Integrating CI with Task Managers

You may want to automate your task management based on the flow of your CI. Most task managers, like Jira and GitHub Project, allow integrations with CI and source control tools. For example, it is possible to use Git commands to move the task state in Kanban. For example:

- A task that is "ready for development" can be moved to "in progress" when a *branch* (in Git) or a *changelist* (in Perforce) with its name is created.

- With each new push on the branch, a continuous integration system is executed.

- When the *pull request* or *swarm review* is created, the task is moved to "in review".

- After, at least, the first approval, the task can be moved to "quality review," which can manually return to "in progress" with additional information on problems found, or add a second approval that allows the branch or changelist to be merged.

- When the work is merged and there is no other branch or changelist with its name open, the task can be moved to "done."

Using Continuous Integration

There is extensive literature on the subject of continuous integration, from books about Agile methodologies to books about software engineering. My goal is to simplify all that for you with the following steps:

1. Developers put the code in their workspaces.

    *   Use git clone [*repository url*] to add the code
        to your workspace.

    *   Use git status to check the status of the code.

2. When changes are ready, you commit them in the
    single repository, usually in a new branch.

    *   Use git checkout -b new-branch to change the
        work branch to new branch.

    *   Use git add -p (using -p to review all changes or
        using . and --all to add everything) to add the
        changes to the commit state.

    *   Use git commit -m "Here goes the comment" to
        commit the changes with comments.

    *   Use git push [*remote-name*][*branch*] (with -f to
        overwrite) to send the changes to the repository.

3. You merge the branch with the main repository.

    *   Use git fetch [*remote*] [*branch*] to search all
        branches of the repository and download all the
        required commits.

    *   Use git merge origin/master to synchronize the
        changes with the master repository.

    *   Instead of the previous commands, you can use git
        pull [*remote*].

4. The CI server monitors the repository and searches
    for changes.

5. The server builds the games and runs the unit and
    integration tests.

6. The server releases an artifact for testing.

7. The server designates a label for the build of the
    version that it is creating.

8. The server informs the team when the build
    completes successfully.

9. If the build or the tests fail, the server warns
    the team.

10. The team fixes the error.

11. You iterate (and continue doing CI).

Tip   Git is a code-versioning system that stores all the code in a
repository. If one of the files on the machine is not necessary for
executing the project, you can use the `.gitignore` command,
which will ignore that file when moving all of them from your
machine to the repository.

You can find more information about GitHub at `https://try.`
`github.io/levels/1/challenges/1`.

A Team's Responsibilities Regarding CI

To implement CI, you need all your team members to meet these
responsibilities:

- *Keep the code updated*: Every time the code needs to be
  edited, it's important that the previous changes have
  already been integrated, especially if they are bug fixes.

- *Do not commit broken code*: Broken code breaks the build and makes it a problem instead of a solution.

- *Do not commit nontested code*: If the code is not tested, there is no guarantee that it is working, and if it's not working, you won't have a working game.

- *Do not commit when the build is broken*: When the build is broken, the last commit should be reversed and fixed. If it's not fixed, future modifications will remain broken, and it won't be possible to identify future problems.

- *Do not abandon the build*: Do not abandon the build until the build of the game is ready. Keep an eye on it, because if it breaks, you'll need to take measures.

So, what about the advantages of using CI in game development?

In addition to the many CI tools that are available and compatible with game development engines, the following are advantages that are important from a time-saving perspective:

- Non-programmers (stakeholders, artists, designers, and technical directors) can test the current version, or older versions, of the game.

- A build with a press release version, something like a short clip of the current state of gameplay in the game, may be made available for release to the media. For example, you can use a bot that does some testing in the game and record the scene.

- The publisher can follow and identify the status of the game.

- You can guarantee that the game runs on different platforms.

- It's easy to get the final version of the build.

- It's easy to fix any bugs that appear in the final version.

Code Versioning

Code versioning provides several benefits because each stage of the code is made available in a system that allows you to identify the strengths of the versions, revert, and divide the code. The following are some advantages of code versioning:

- *You changed the code and realized it was a mistake*: Just reverse it. If the commit has already gone to build, it's a best practice to revert and redo.

- *You lost the code and the backup version is too old*: Just commit frequently. If commits are made often, you won't have any problems restoring lost code.

- *You need to check the differences in code versions*: Use git diff. Many versioning tools allow you to check the differences between the code in progress and the original. Another advantage is that you can check out the modification log, allowing you to identify when a feature was added.

- *You need to identify which change broke the code*: Code versioning facilitates the identification and fixing of faulty changes. You just identify in the CI platform which commit broke the code. Furthermore, this is related to the previous topic because it includes the concept of verifying differences.

- *You can divide the work over the code*: Work division is important in large projects so that the development can be done concurrently, not in sequence.

- *You can follow the development of the code*: The visualization of the project progress allows the development team to check the progress of the game. It also allows outside people to check how things are going.

- *You can keep different versions of a product*: Many times it's necessary to keep the build from different platforms. Continuous integration allows you to do that in a simple way. One way to do it is by using branches.

Note   It's a best practice to use comments on commits that identify which task/work/ticket generated the modification and what was done. When a branch is created, it should identify which task the branch belongs to and what it will do.

All these difficulties can be solved with versioning. My preference and suggestion is to implement versioning through Git, such as with GitHub.

For Unity, remember that the steps are similar to other tools. For instance, here are the steps to version your code:

1. Use gitignore.io to generate your version, avoiding sending hundreds of unnecessary files to the build. Watch out for 3D models ending in .obj because you must exclude .[Oo]bj models from this file.

2. In Editor Settings, under Asset Serialization Mode, select Force Text Flag. This prevents the Unity files from being sent as binaries because that may create merge issues on GitHub. It's complex to do a merge of numerical sequences.

3. In Editor Settings, under Version Control Mode, select Visible Meta Files. The metafiles are important for the Unity project to locate its parts.

Automated Build

Let's use Unity Engine as the example. It has an internal system that allows automated builds, called the Unity Cloud Build,[1] as well as a support system for other CIs, called the GameCI.[2] Unreal has Unreal Containers[3] and Bevy Engine uses Rust's native systems for CI.

In cases where the automated build is not part of the engine, I believe it will be less of a headache to use an existing system. In a quick Google search for the terms "CI" and "Games," I came across several references to Jenkins, CircleCI, and TravisCI. All are very common and versatile to apply in games; just use an engine that has containers.

In addition, there's TeamCity (`www.jetbrains.com/teamcity/`), which is optimized for C#. For other software, there are other sources, such as Go CI and Snap CI. Of these, Jenkins is probably the most popular for doing automated builds in games; it's a simple platform to use to implement jobs, and it has an active community.

---

[1] `https://unity3d.com/learn/tutorials/topics/cloud-build/introduction-unity-cloud-build`

[2] `https://game.ci/`

[3] `https://unrealcontainers.com/docs/use-cases/continuous-integration`

Most importantly, your code is built in a single step. Depending on your level of proficiency in CI, it is possible to build on the most diverse platforms in a single automated step, as well as run all the tests on different platforms in parallel.

An important part of automating processes is ensuring uniformity and ensuring that all tests run the same way. This applies both to the automation of unit tests, which can be run before the build stage, and to the functional testing stage. For those using Unity, I suggest unit tests with NUnit and NSubstitute and functional and integration tests with Unity Test Runner. Make your build self-testing, and fast.

Summary

In this chapter, you learned about the value of CI, as well as how and where to use it. You also saw how to use CI in games. Most importantly, you learned how CI can be very helpful in a market that typically presents a lot of bugs. With this information in hand, you can start to think about designing and building a game.

CHAPTER 9

The World Between Design and Build

Chapter 2 covered the first steps of using Lean and briefly mentioned design and build. It also covered tools that help with the Agile process. The goal of this chapter is to explain these concepts in depth and discuss how to use them in Lean game development.

According to Vitor Leães, professor of the specialization in digital game development at Pontifical Catholic University of Rio Grande do Sul (PUCRS):

> *The biggest challenge in the production of a video game is to seek alignment between several extremely different disciplines: game design itself, engineering, visual design and art, marketing, writing and narrative. For this, managers, producers, and leaders need to master a range of methods and "ways of doing" that go far beyond Agile. I'm a Scrum fan, but I don't believe that its purist application meets all the needs of the game development process. I've managed art teams on many projects and I understand that the initial stage (preproduction) is the most uncertain and often frustrating: finding the look of the game, its face, validating whether it meets the profile of the target audience, of the genre, compare it with the other games in the same segment to be close but, at the same time, innovative. This can be extremely complex, and the team often feels like it's going in circles, but it's a necessary time. After a*

© Julia Naomi Rosenfield Boeira 2024
J. N. Rosenfield Boeira, *Lean Game Development*,
https://doi.org/10.1007/978-1-4842-9843-5_9

well-done preproduction, where all styles, and creative and art production processes are defined, the level of uncertainty in the project with regard to art is greatly reduced. In this way, it is possible to start with a waterfall production model, just focusing on listing the amount of art assets needed to create the game's content and distribute them to the art team, in a sort of "line of production."

Generally, *design* is responsible for predicting what the software is going to be (from the artistic and visual parts to the user experience), and *build* refers to how you are going to develop the idealized design and what is and isn't possible to do.

Tip   To help distinguish design from build, you can think of it like this: "Design makes the recipe, and build prepares the meal." It's the difference between planning and doing. Design's concern is with utility, and build's concern is with the technical specifications and tools.

A Little Bit of Design

Formulating the game design involves a series of iterations and can also be a moment to reflect on whether it's worth continuing the project. However, this is not its main function.

An important task during the design phase is to search for information about the needs and the utility of the project. Many times, it's necessary to ask random people what they think about the project and/or create prototypes and board games that try to simulate, as precisely as possible, the mechanics and features of the game to be developed. This allows you to determine if the game is viable and has potential.

An efficient design allows for a minimum waste of resources and time. Design is the step in which the project's elements are prioritized and the team tries to eliminate strict specifications because they are costly to modify. Hence, everything that can be decided in another iteration must be left for the next iteration. Remember that leaving something for later doesn't mean you will not do it. It means that you should not get stressed now about something that shouldn't be solved yet, that cannot be solved, that is blocked for any reason, and so on.

For the design to be a success, it's necessary to think of many elements of the game, including the following: the game set, the characters, the features and mechanics, the kind of experience you want users to have, the plot, and its gameplay. Think about a *Castlevania*-style scene in which a character is playing the piano: is it worth it to make a super-complete animation or something minimally realistic about the character playing the piano? You make important decisions in the design stage that can affect the build stage.

A Little Bit of Build

What about the build? The *build* is the step in which all information solidified in the design stage is used to start thinking about the development process. You must remember that, in games, developing also includes creating artwork and sound effects (and their iterations), if these elements were decided on during design. However, they are not something you should worry about at this time.

If the solutions suggested in the build stage are not good, you will realize in the next iteration because the concepts need to be developed in the ideation, hypotheses, and design phases. That is, during the build, you can discuss some style and development specifications, and, if needed, you can step backward. It's important that development keeps the pace of the code and is continuously integrated because it's a creative process that changes over time and feedback is important.

For instance, take a game that has a scene in which the character turns their back and starts to play the piano. Say the artist got excited and animated the whole scene of the character playing the piano, but the fingers are never seen. That would be easily prevented if the artist would have used prototyping and continuous delivery; also a lot of memory would have been spared. In the build, you can define which unit tests are going to be run, clarify how the functional tests are going to be developed, and observe whether some programming pattern emerges. You basically specify how all of these things are going to be delivered, automated, tested, and integrated.

Pretty Beautiful, But How Is It Done?

First of all, we have *MVG Zero,* a board game[1]—"I love planning a game as a board game first." This is the time to determine if the overall game mechanics and features are interesting, fun, and coherent—and, if not, to try to identify how you can improve them. Creating a board game usually requires a lot of creativity and allows all teams to envision what they want to have as a product.

The board game we designed consists of a board divided in tabular form: the lower part of the game is formed by non-interactive spaces (the ground) and spaces that can cause the death of the player (the holes). Enemy behavior is generated by a random value (die result) each turn. Since we wanted a 2D platform game, we used a projection onto tabular paper with blocks and characters printed in a horizontal orthogonal projection (instead of the vertical orthogonal projection traditionally used in board games).

---

[1] Marc LeBlanc is a huge proponent of early board game design. Some of his work can be found at https://users.cs.northwestern.edu/~hunicke/pubs/MDA.pdf and https://www.gamedesignworkshop.com/marc-leblanc

The main character can move freely according to the dice, but a jump costs one extra dice unit. This is the same as in *Mario,* when you determine that killing enemies implies falling over them; so, if the character stands over the enemy, it dies. Enemies can move from -3 to 3 positions horizontally. To win the game, three lives are enough.

Creating the board game requires several tiny cycles that you can do in a Lean way and finish quickly, with no great artistic complications. Figure 9-1 shows *MVG Zero,* a board game prototype. I can assure you it was fun to build and provided plenty of game hours.

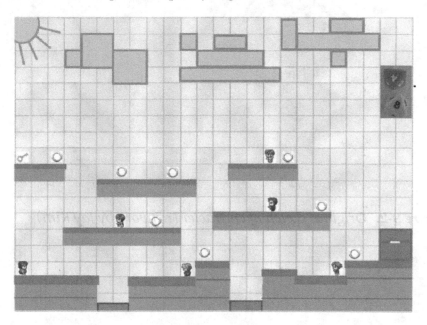

Figure 9-1. *Board game prototype*

Considering that this model has eight prototypes that form MVG and three delivery cycles, and knowing that each iteration corresponds to a prototype, we therefore had to do at least eight iterations. We had the initial hypotheses, but we also had to ideate for the next iterations, generating new ideas.

In the first stage of design, you define the narrative of the first MVG so that the PO can guide the game vision and indicate how you want the mechanics of the prototype to look. Figures 9-2 through 9-5 represent the idealizations of how mechanics work in the example and some conceptual artwork for MVG's prototypes.

Figure 9-2. *Original sketch of character (artwork by Jay Kim)*

Figure 9-3. *Original sketch of the movement mechanics*

Figure 9-4. *Original sketch of the jump mechanics*

Figure 9-5. *Original sketch of the fall mechanics*

Figure 9-6 shows the pixel art that resulted from the sketches.

Figure 9-6. *Character sprite sheet (artwork by Jay Kim)*

What about the build? How are you going to do the tests? What tools
are going to be used? How animations are going to be made? And the
sprites? How much time do you project this iteration to take? How is
everything going to be integrated? How will you deliver? Who are you
going to pair up with? Where will you do the code versioning? Is what
you have still valid? Does it work? Is it worth migrating? These are the
questions that Figures 9-7 through 9-9 answer.

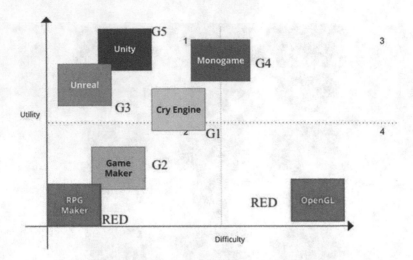

Figure 9-7. *Game development tools*

Tests are explained in the tables of the next chapter. Figure 9-7 shows the tool preferences for game development: the dark green color (G5) indicates the favorite tool, the light green (G1) indicates the least favorite, and the red color means tools to be excluded. Figure 9-8 shows preferences for integration tools (if this project was complete today, we would probably have gone with GitHub Actions). Also, I decided to use the pixel tool to generate the sprites shown in Figure 9-6 and animate via Unity.

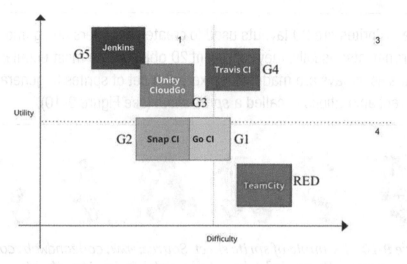

Figure 9-8. *Integration tools*

Figure 9-9 represents the idealization of the possible stages of continuous delivery. The code versioning was done via GitHub. I didn't have any valid existing code for this game; however, I used some old experimental code.

Continuous Delevery

Board Game	Simple Prototype	Complete Prototype	Final Prototype	Art Demo	Marketing Release	Internal Alpha Testing
External Alpha Testing	Beta	Early Launch	Public Launch	Cross Plataform	Updates ...	

Figure 9-9. *Continuous delivery sequencer for the game*

Note   Sprites are 2D layouts used to create characters and game environments; usually, they represent 2D objects. The most popular sprites nowadays are made with pixel art. A set of sprites to generate different animations is called a *sprite sheet* (see Figure 9-10).

Figure 9-10. *Example of sprite sheet. Source:* www.codeandweb.com/ texturepacker/tutorials/how-to-create-a-sprite-sheet

Tip   A good sprite editor is Piskel (see Figure 9-11). It allows you to generate sprites pixel by pixel, with many colors and tools (www. piskelapp.com/).

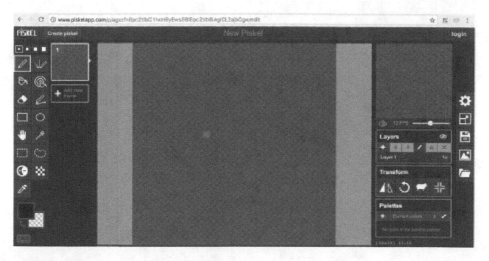

Figure 9-11. *Sprite editor Piskel*

Summary

Now you know the fundamental differences between the design and build stages. You learned about the expectations of each stage and saw one interesting example of concept usability. Now that everything has been defined, you can move on to the most pleasurable parts: coding and testing.

CHAPTER 10

Test, Code, Test

One of the most important steps when a building game is writing the code and testing it. Although a game is artistic software, it still needs to be coded and tested. Therefore, this chapter explains what kinds of tests can be performed, how to elaborate on test cases, and how to automate this process for code and art.

What is the best way to start this process?

The game design is done, but how do you turn the game design into a game with the least number of possible bugs? You can use software development techniques such as test-driven development (TDD) and extreme programming (XP). It's not absolutely necessary to follow the development techniques, and adaptations are always welcome, but it's important to use them as guidance in development. One of the most important lessons you can get from them is the fact that testing is important. That's why you need to test from the start.

Testing Types

When you think of development, a series of questions probably arise regarding testing. For this specific feature, how will you do the tests? What is the simplest test? What will the step-by-step process be for the test? What about test automation? How will that be done?

© Julia Naomi Rosenfield Boeira 2024
J. N. Rosenfield Boeira, *Lean Game Development*,
https://doi.org/10.1007/978-1-4842-9843-5_10

All those questions must be answered and planned in the build stage so that the coding and testing stages go as well as possible. The following are some types of tests:

- *Unit test*: This type of test checks one unit, one feature, or one routine developed by the programmer. A good test would be to ensure that, for example, by pressing the X button, the character receives a jump command. These are the classic assert tests in TDD examples.

- *Functional test*: This test ensures that the functionality of a class or namespace is satisfied.

- *Component test*: This type of test runs a class, a package, or a small software program that involves the work of many programmers or a team of programmers. A good example is when a state machine is tested in several ways.

- *Integration test*: This is a test between two or more classes, namespaces, packages, components, or systems. It starts when two different classes/ namespaces interact. A good example is when Mario falls on a Koopa to guarantee that the Koopa will become a shell and "roll away."

- *Regression test*: This is a continuous integration test that looks for defects not found earlier with different versions. It's a sort of contract test that ensures that a great set of features and its integrations will work no matter what the version is. In games, it can ensure that side-effects are controlled.

- *System test (game)*: This test runs the software in its final configuration. It tests all possible solutions and interactions. Something like an *end-to-end test,* in

which you generate a bot that allows you to test all
the possible features of the game (a technique often
used to generate gameplays). In the gaming industry,
it is known as *gameplay testing* and is commonly
developed by QAs (quality analysts) or dev testers,
who unfortunately end up doing manual tests over and
over again.

- *Smoke test (gameplay)*: This is similar to a system/
  game test, but is usually executed in gyms or in a more
  controlled environment so that the gameplay mechanic
  can be tested with specific data.

Test Cases

Let's begin with a simple example that does not apply specifically to the
game market but that most developers have to face at some point. Imagine
that your team has to develop a feature for a company that uses a bank
system. The feature must check a credit card number to ensure that the
number entered is valid. Table 10-1 presents the case.

Table 10-1. *Test Cases for Features*

Feature	Test the Validity of a Credit Card
Input	A string representing the credit card number and two numbers to represent the month and year of the expiration date.
Tests	1. Check whether all the bytes in the string are digits.
	2. Check whether the month number is between 1 and 12.
	3. Check whether the year is later than the current year.
	4. Check whether the four first digits of the card are from a valid issuer.
	5. Check whether the system is valid in an external system.
Output	OK, or error with message indication that the card is not valid.

The following are the test strategies recommended for developers:

- Test each requirement or feature, ensuring that the entire codebase is tested and verifying the quality of the code. In addition, tests must be established in the build stage so they favor development and enable what must be done during development. Extra tests are also welcomed.

- Start with base tests, which are fundamental units for the code's operation. Then move on to more detailed and specific tests that represent more complex components and features.

- Each line of logic code must be tested. This is the only way to ensure the continuous integrity throughout the game's development; it's also a great way to create documentation.

- List all the errors in the project to monitor your performance and improve your technique. This is a way to accomplish personal development.

- Write the tests before starting to code. Besides being a best practice in programming, this technique almost guarantees that you don't write more code than is necessary.

- Work to create clean tests. Summing up, this consists of keeping the test and the code comprehensible and simple—to a level of KISS.

- Review your work.

Note   Keep It Simple, Stupid (KISS) is a general principle that values the simplicity of the project and recommends that all unnecessary complexity is discarded (see `https://en.wikipedia.org/wiki/KISS_principle`).

Coding Game Artwork

Coding can involve much more than writing the actual code to make an application work. Coding can also mean creating, because the artwork needs to be developed at this time and will also be tested. Because the artwork goes through a creative process that cannot be test-driven, it's a little more difficult to apply the TDD principles to artistic areas. However, the concept of art in games is more technical and commercial than a pure artistic expression, and thus allows you, at least, to test the functionality and people's reaction to the art object.

In addition, many times the artistic creation process is something very subjective, so different people will respond in different ways to different stimuli. A solution for this is to focus on the smallest artistic units possible.

Let's look at the *Jujuba* example. To test the game's code, you don't need great art; you just need a set of blocks and other geometrical shapes that can give you the feeling that you are playing with a character—you saw some of this in Chapter 5, when you learned about the first prototypes of *Horizon Zero Dawn*. However, when testing the vertical slice of the MVG, you should consider this art validation to be more holistic and analyze it collectively. An example here is when color and shape language are used, then artistic elements like lighting and props can hinder or destroy the original intent. For example, color language was used to communicate game state, but when lighting was added, it shifted the colors that the player saw, thus muddling or destroying the original intent and confusing the players.

Another important point is that the creative process shouldn't be interrupted. Although I agree that artistic inspiration shouldn't be interrupted, many games have suffered from artistic block. An example is *FEZ*, an indie game developed by Phil Fish. The point that I am emphasizing here is that not every step of artistic creation must be free in all senses.

In this case, you already know who you want to reach because the audience was identified when you defined the personas. Furthermore, you must choose your priorities, which is a great way to allow your brain to think about what you want and what you can do with what you conceived.

So, what about an artistic design driven by tests? First, you should remember that you have a clear separation of priorities in the prototype; thus, you shouldn't be worried about what you still haven't done. At the first stage, you should simply work with the prototyped shape of what you want.

Because the first prototype tends to be shorter than the others, perhaps you can simply make a humanoid with long hair and basic clothes. You don't have to attend to details or determine the best way to portray a character; just provide a good, basic starting point.

Do you want to test this prototype? As art is subjective, you can test by asking for feedback and explaining that it's a prototype. List the similar feedback and check whether the information matches your priorities. If it doesn't, maybe you'll use a parking lot (explained in Appendix A). If it does, you can apply the necessary changes, and from now on, you'll have a harmonious, elegant, artistic, and tested prototype.

Note   What about using automated tests on your artwork? I haven't seen much work on this yet. However, you could use image recognition software and machine learning to validate animations, shapes, coloring, lighting, and scenes.

Coding the Game Software

You should now have a clear idea as to what should be coded first: your prototype. You can use the following tables as a guide for how every step should be completed. Remember, during the build stage, you decided which tests were going to be made for each feature you were creating for the first prototype.

Although I have already defined the stages of prototypes, they can be broken into other stages and restructured using the feedback and ideation process. The features for the prototypes are walk, jump, and fall, as listed in Tables 10-2 through 10-4.

Table 10-2. *Developing the Walking Feature*

Feature	Character Should Walk Toward the X-Axis
Input	Keyboard inputs.
Tests	1. Check whether a specific key is being pressed.
	2. Check whether the direction keys (left and right) are being pressed.
	3. Check that when the left direction key is pressed, the character moves to the left.
	4. Check that when the right direction key is pressed, the character moves to the right.
	5. Check whether the other keys, when pressed, don't move the character (in many cases, you can exclude the keys ASWD).
	6. Check whether the character collides with the end of the scenery.
Output	If the new position is as expected, the test passes; otherwise, it fails.

Table 10-3. *Development of Walking Feature*

Feature	Character Should Jump
Input	Keyboard inputs.
Tests:	1. Check whether the spacebar is being pressed for jumping.
	2. Check that when the key is pressed, the character moves up one position.
	3. Check whether the character moves softly from the bottom to the top (check for two or more points in the first part of the jump).
	4. Check whether the character moves softly from the top to the bottom (a complete jump).
	5. Check that when a direction key is pressed, the jump is in the same direction.
	6. Check whether the jump makes a parabola (five points at least).
Output	If the new position is as expected, the test passes; otherwise, it fails.

Table 10-4.   *Development of Falling Feature*

Feature	Character Should Fall When There Are Holes in the Scenery
Input	Character collides with the scenery.
Tests	1. Check whether the character collides with parts of the ground.
	2. Check whether the character collides with air blocks in the scenery.
	3. Check whether the character falls when there is a hole in the ground.
	4. Check whether the character falls by making a horizontal launch affected by gravity from the ground.
	5. Check whether the character falls by making a horizontal launch affected by gravity from an air block.
Output	If the new position or new state is as expected, the test passes; otherwise, it fails.

Note   The examples presented in the tables correspond to the tests created for the first prototype of the *Super Jujuba Sisters* game.

Each programmer can conceptualize differently how these tests are going to be made, but the important point is to keep the coding simple and the solution even simpler. If a step is too vague or obscure, conceiving of and running an intermediate test can be a good solution. In addition, any deeper modification, such as refactoring and class extraction, can become much less laborious after fixing errors via tests.

In software development, it's common to update application versions, including games, after release. Identifying broken tests and differences between what was expected and what was found can be a great way to optimize the code, with no need to review the whole logic. Furthermore, it's much simpler to understand what the code should do when tests document what should happen. Always start with the simplest and most fundamental test to guarantee that the minimum planned task is happening.

Test Automation

Unit and integration tests developed by the programmer are a great source for starting automation because they are fundamental for checking whether the features are working properly. Therefore, it's important to automate the process in which this is done.

A *test runner* is a tool that allows you to run a sequence of all kinds of tests from a command line. In the case of Unity, the test runner provides integration between tests and the visual output, allowing the programmer to verify what is going on. Figure 10-1 shows a visual test runner, followed by an example of the commands you can run. The following are some test automation components you should know about:

- *Test manager*: This component manages the operation of the software tests. It also keeps a record of the test data and the expected results.

- *Test data generator*: This component generates data that must be tested by the software. It can use predefined patterns or random data required for specific stages of the game.

- *Expected data generator*: This component's main function is to generate all possible data for an automated test, such as end-to-end data.

- *Results comparator*: This component's main function is to compare new results and old ones.

- *Report generator*: This component generates reports on test results.

- *Dynamic analyst*: This component sees and counts function calls made by the code.

- *Simulator*: This component simulates user interactions with different types of systems, such as testing different platforms.

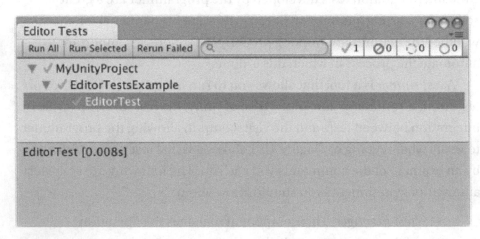

Figure 10-1. *Command-line test runner for Unity. Source:* `https://docs.unity3d.com/Manual/testing-editortestsrunner.html`

The following command allows you to execute the engine and the tests without user input. It's a test runner that runs from the command line. (See `https://docs.unity3d.com/Manual/testing-editortestsrunner.html`.)

```
Unity.exe -runTests -batchmode  -projectPath </path/to/project>
-testResults C:\temp\results.xml -testPlatform PS4. -batchmode
```

Summary

In this chapter, you learned what to do before coding, namely, you define the tests and the development policies. In addition, you learned about some great tools so you can use to implement best practices in tests. Next, you need to focus on getting what you have already integrated by learning about metrics.

CHAPTER 11

Measuring and Analyzing

You've learned all about iterating and you understand that you need ways to measure and analyze the results of iterations. Therefore, the first step is to be able to measure the results that your iteration obtained and continue to generate ideas from these results. In practice, your goal should be to maximize learning through iterations and, therefore, develop better quality and safer products each new iteration.

Ways to Measure

A very common way to measure hypotheses and results is to hire companies that specialize in games to deliver a report with feedback about the game. This model consists of allowing them to play a demo, alpha, beta, or even each release. They create reports about the current state of the game. These companies, in addition to having a positive advertising impact, can contribute great recommendations and feedback. But what makes the difference is what you do with this information. The only problem is the price of the service, which is quite high and can make it unfeasible to test each new release. Some of these companies specialize in collecting user feedback after a soft launch as well. Many smaller studios prefer to do this on their own, which is valid, but requires some expertise to deliver a great feedback report.

© Julia Naomi Rosenfield Boeira 2024
J. N. Rosenfield Boeira, *Lean Game Development*,
https://doi.org/10.1007/978-1-4842-9843-5_11

It is important to remember that, during all stages of development, it is necessary to measure how the product is doing. Therefore, you need to look for ways to receive qualitative information—keeping in mind that the dev's view of how the game is doing is usually biased. If you don't want to hire a third-party[1] company to collect feedback, you should aim to collect the most feedback you can from all areas (teams, users, market, clients, media, etc.), prioritize that feedback, and work on it.

Here are some examples of measurement that I've seen:

- *Try to collect opinions and ideas from team members:* Despite being developers, team contributors also tend to play games. Their insights and suggestions can be very helpful to the game's development.

- *Hold demo testing sessions*: Many people wait in line for hours to test demo games. A good way to measure this is to launch demos at events and analyze people's reactions to the game, as well as collect feedback. Gamescon is often used for this purpose. One tip I've learned is to record the user screen, controls, and faces and then have your UX team analyze this information to identify players' satisfaction.

- *Feedback*: This chapter dives deep into this topic.

- *Validate hypotheses*: This chapter also dives deep into this topic.

---

[1] Even third-party feedback can be improperly interpreted. Proper data analysis practices should be followed. Many game companies have made costly decisions by improperly evaluating tons of skewed data. A data scientist can help organize and evaluate the data.

- *Analytics*: There are several ways to collect data. Using this data to improve the gaming experience is a great way to measure satisfaction.

I have two examples of analytics feedback:

- **Call of Duty Black Ops 2:** This game had a ton of weapons performance modifications, as well as new weapons being created, resulting in a better balance of properties. An example of this is that they decreased the damage of the FAL weapon and created a new weapon in the DLC (extra downloadable content).

- **Starlit:** This game, by Rockhead, is a great example, as it managed to captivate my son for hours at a time. The Rockhead team looked at the average performance of players in certain regions. When it was too easy, they made it difficult; when it was too difficult, they facilitated or improved the gaming experience. In my opinion, this is one of the best ways to measure.

Analytics

Analytics is the discovery, interpretation, and communication of meaningful patterns in data. It can be used to describe, predict, and improve business/game performance. For games, it's a powerful tool to understand the behavior of players, providing valuable insights about them and the game (see Figure 11-1). Some analytics options include the following:

- Game Analytics: `https://github.com/GameAnalytics`

- Unity: `https://www.assetstore.unity3d.com/en/#!/content/6755`

Figure 11-1. *Example of game analytics*

Measuring Through Feedback

Feedback can be of several types, but the main ones, especially in games, are reactions to a game clip or gameplay, or a person's performance in a task. They aim to improve the product or people's performance. Feedback can be given continuously or when relevant situations occur. It is important to maintain the feedback culture, as its objective is to improve personal performance or product quality. You must always be looking for feedback, whether asking for it from customers and users or looking for it in forums. Another important tip for handling feedback is to not get too attached to the product. Lastly, when talking about the product, it is important to keep evaluation practices as scientific as possible, so make predictions based on actual data and large samples, then the change conditions and retest.

One of the ways to receive game feedback is through Twitter, Discord, Reddit, or Steam accounts. A well-developed habit in the game dev community is having active accounts where people post pictures, comment on their new releases, and at the same time receive feedback from customers/users, companies, and other game developers. Another way is to encourage the entire team to actively participate in collecting feedback throughout the game's development, whether through feedback from the PO, from business and marketing analysts, or from other developers. This active search for feedback has another important effect on the players—it shows that the developer is concerned about the opinion of the target audience, which creates a very cool sense of community. Something that was crucial to *Dead Cells'* development.

A very interesting example of using feedback and proximity to the community to develop new features was in the Senna Forever expansion of the *Horizon Chase* game, by Aquiris. A playtest group was created with fans of the game who were active on the game's Discord. This resulted in an expansion pack with a sense of co-building from the community. That sense of belonging can be a huge motivator, especially as it tries to find its niche. I have seen more games fail to find their niche (or find "the fun") than games that have been successful.

As for team members, it's important to keep feedback polite and sincere. Try not to insert personal issues and keep them reasonable. When taken seriously, feedback can improve performance and fix small bugs—which we all have.

What's Feedback?

Feedback is an important tool for understanding how people perceive your game, which behaviors you can improve upon, and which ones you should keep and even emphasize.

Note   *Feedback* is a suggestion to reinforce or improve a certain point.

Good feedback is based on three main points: the data noticed about a fact, the story you built around it, and the argument you had to get to the conclusion. Take a look at the following example to make things clearer:

Felipe Says   "In the update you gave in the meeting today, I think you were not clear enough. It seems you were distracted."

Julia Says   "Thank you, Felipe. I hadn't noticed that. I'll be more careful."

How to Give Feedback[2]

The following are some important points to consider before giving someone feedback:

- *Start the conversation*: Look for a calm place to talk, such as a coffee house. Avoid unnecessary tension.

- *Ideal environment*: it's important to have the discussion alone. More people participating in the conversation than necessary can generate tension.

- *Set the objectives of the conversation*: Be clear why you are having this conversation and why you believe it will help the other person.

---

[2] These tips about feedback were taken from Felipe de Moraes' blog (https://medium.com/@felipedemoraes) with permission and translated from Portuguese.

- *Describe the feedback clearly*: It's always good to remind the person about the situation that generated the feedback and explain the conclusion you came to in the moment. This is the moment to talk about what you need, and remember to always tell how the feedback could help the other person.

- *Validate the feedback*: Check whether the person agrees, and open some room for questioning. There's no need for others to agree on what was said, though.

- *Avoid bad vibes*: It's time to have empathy and sense how the person is reacting to the feedback. If the person takes it badly, remind them that your goal was to help them.

- *Give the feedback sooner rather than later*: The longer it's been since the incident, the less likely the person will remember what happened, and thus the less impactful the feedback will be.

Measuring Through Hypotheses

Some chapters ago, I talked about hypotheses and how they can help you measure and test your minimum viable games (MVGs), prototypes, and increments. However, up to now, you are not using your hypotheses to get results. Results go way beyond simple data, because data can be collected partially; you need to be searching out good data and avoid negative data, which will affect the data's results.

You need ways to measure your hypotheses so that they give you information that generates knowledge, whether for good or bad, to provide you with future insights. In fact, you will turn your ideas and insights into hypotheses to be evaluated in the future.

Basically, hypotheses allow you to evaluate results since they're the ideas that will be tested and can be modified only in the next iteration, which will occur after analysis and learning. Using all the information and feedback you collected, you can test hypotheses without selecting data and keeping your judgment as neutral as possible.

I think this is an important moment to remind you that the goal of game companies is not to only make money but also to provide great experiences and entertainment. Evan Boehler said, "We make money by making great experiences."[3] So, if your hypotheses are based on financial metrics, there's a good chance your game will fail or will not be innovative and fun. Many large companies fail because they keep their metrics purely financial, and they end up making their games and characters extremely repetitive and not innovative.

A result of evaluating hypotheses is knowing your clients and knowing the possible impact the game will have on the market. Validating hypotheses is dealing with risks, because it is much easier to develop when you think that everything is right than to develop while observing the failures. The hypothesis model so far is described as follows:

We believe that by building the feature **[name of the feature/ prototype]** for the **[intended audience]**, we will achieve **[the expected results]**.

We know that we are successful when we have **[the expected market sign]**.

---

[3] "If making money is your goal, you'll just make a boring uninspired game. Too many companies are just trying to make money and all making the same mistakes."

You know the audience you want to impact, the outcome you want to get with the MVG or the prototype, and the metric you set as an expected sign of this success. With this information, you can determine whether your target audience has given you the expected sign of your outcome through the feedback and analytics, for instance. In addition, sales data and downloads can contribute to feedback. However, they tend to be cloudier regarding the target audience since many users are not used to making their personal data public or they might even use false data. Comments on the game page in online stores or on Twitter, Reddit, and Discord accounts can also be powerful tools in validating hypotheses through feedback. With these signed measures, whether positive, negative, complex or simple, you can prepare for the next step: "How can you perform analysis on your metrics and hypotheses?"

Analyzing

When analyzing, you need to remain as impartial as possible. The more information and results that are available from the metric validation, the more important and relevant the analysis will be. While the importance of analysis increases with the quality and quantity of data, the complexity and the advantages increase as well.

Therefore, when you analyze, you must classify the types of feedback, data, and metrics you used to develop your hypotheses so you can keep adding to those categories in the future. The measures resulting from metrics—from MVGs, prototypes, and increments to features and to mechanics—allow you to identify points that you need to improve.

After this stage, you can separate the categories by relevance or by impact on the game development. This allows you to analyze how much revision is needed and where you need to improve the product/game. It's also important to remember that much of the feedback is disconnected from the necessities of the game or the team. The feedback can be useful many times but not at the moment. Thus, it's worth it to leave the feedback in the parking lot (see Appendix A) to be used later.

During analysis, it's important to compare the feedback with the stories and personas you generated previously, in addition to being clear on what information you want to get from the analysis. The metrics of hypotheses allow you to verify if the MVG/prototype/increment, the feature, or the mechanic is adequate. This allows you to improve the game in the next stage and generate a continuous improvement process.

Measuring Your Hypothesis of the Female Audience Reach

Consider this hypothesis from Chapter 6:

"We believe that by building a strong non-stereotypical female character, with interesting gameplay functions, we will be able to reach the female audience, who will be excited by our game. We know that we have been successful when lots of girls start to comment in our feed."

This hypothesis is way beyond mechanics and features. It introduces aesthetic concepts of the game and an audience usually left aside, especially in Japanese games. Is promoting the character and the game at the same time a good way to be successful? You can verify this is working if, when the newly released game does not have many downloads from women, but later, after a few speeches, videos, and tweets about it, you have a legion of fans.

This would be a proper metric if that was your intention with the hypothesis; however, you are seeking to hear direct feedback and generate discussions. If your feedback and discussions don't appear in the metrics, you may have to rethink what you got with the hypothesis.

- The character was empathic with the female audience but not enough to engage manifestations.

- You are not available to get feedback.

- There was a failure in communicating the intention.

- You didn't reach your audience.

- The kind of game was not directed at your audience (I think that every game category can be adaptable to all audiences, though).

- The audience loved it, and the game is a success! (This never happens to 100 percent of the audience)

Tip   You must analyze every comment seriously, whether it represents 2 percent or 100 percent of the total. However, you have to prioritize the most common and the most relevant feedback from the team's point of view, yet, as much as possible, try to analyze the other feedback.

Measuring Your Hypotheses on Basic Features

"We believe that building the features of walking, jumping, and falling into the game will result in a game with strong basic mechanics. We know that we have been successful when we have positive feedback from manual tests and from third parties through the demo we will have."

This hypothesis is a little bit deceiving because you know that many games are based on these mechanics and can be successful unexpectedly. Of course, game testers will focus on features from a technical point of view, so, even if have fun, their goal is to see whether the game works. This is relevant information because if, from the testers' point of view, the game is not working, you should take action to fix it.

Now imagine sharing a demo of the game with random people, or better, sharing demos with slight differences in features to different groups of people and measuring which of the demos was best received. Using these situations, you can develop the following analyses:

- The features of the game are bad and must be fixed.

- The playability of the game is bad, and the project must be rethought.

- The features are okay, but the game is not fun.

- The game is fun but very hard to play.

- The critiques were great!

Thinking like this, you can get a set of possible signs about your hypotheses that allow you to go to the next stage with clear measures, such as feedback on game mechanics and features and analytics on the player performance in different sections of the game. These measures allow you to analyze strong and weak points of features to be validated by hypotheses and allow you to think through problems, solutions, and points of action. With points of action in mind, you can go to the next stage: ideations over action to be taken.

A very good way is to send demos to YouTubers, streamers, and other game influencers for them to review, even if the demos have other names or project codes. Pick a serious YouTuber and they will review the game from an entertainment and quality point of view. You could even send slightly different demos to each tester and measure their reactions to the differences.

Summary

In the beginning of this chapter, you learned about the core concepts of feedback and learned how to give feedback. Feedback is important in Lean development, because it can be the core measure to iterate on your project. You also saw some different ways to measure game results, especially analytics tools. You saw how to validate and get results from hypotheses. Lastly, you saw some examples of analyzing using the hypotheses developed in previous chapters.

CHAPTER 12

Creating Ideas for Iterating

Before iterating, it's necessary to come up with ideas about what you need to improve in the next stage and understand which feedback and hypotheses results can be used to improve your game. After measuring and analyzing, you need to use all the generated information. This stage is called *ideation*, which is similar to inception, but much shorter and more focused. Also, during the ideation stage, you have a lot more information about the game because it is already being developed. The stage can validate the current hypotheses and generate ground-breaking ideas for developing the game. Ideation can also generate new hypotheses and help you rethink the design and build steps so that the game development process will be quicker and better.

Action Items

Each action item needs an explanatory title and a description. Furthermore, you need to present what generated the item, including the involved feature, the base hypothesis, and the identified sign. It's also a good idea to include a brief description of the reason for creating the action item, and even assign someone to do it.

© Julia Naomi Rosenfield Boeira 2024
J. N. Rosenfield Boeira, *Lean Game Development*,
https://doi.org/10.1007/978-1-4842-9843-5_12

While generating ideas, it may be useful to bring up the inception concept. However, this time it can be shorter and more focused because you already have the minimum viable products (MVPs). At this point, ideation improves the concepts of MVPs, as well as helps generate new hypotheses and perfects the concepts of the game in general.

The ideation process consists of brainstorming with the previous data and generating adaptation propositions for MVPs, without losing the focus and the vision of the game. It's important to keep your judgments impartial at this point and to think "out-of-the-box," perhaps using techniques that stimulate creativity. The ideation stage is one of the best ways to find solutions to the problems identified in the measurement and analysis stages. During this stage, the recommendation is to have the most diverse profiles because that's the only way to gather a variety of ideas.

To organize the suggestions, you can use an *ideas menu*, which is a synthesis of the ideas generated so far, with the goal of ordering the insights and making them visible and comprehensible to everybody. A good way to deal with the problem is to use a *sketching session*, which is a way to get the team more involved in design decisions, create a deeper understanding, and consider the end users. It also helps to define the problem and propose improvements.

SKETCHING SESSION

The **[game/feature]** is **[what is intended]**.

So that **[players/users]** can **[goals of users]**, we note that **[current problem/limitation of the current system]**, which makes **[reason of being a problem]**.

How can you **[what to solve]** so that **[benefit of solving]**?

Example of a Sketching Session

In the previous chapter, the following hypothesis was used to generate metrics:

> *"We believe that building the features of walking, jumping, and falling into the game will result in a game with strong basic mechanics. We know that we have been successful when we have positive feedback from manual tests and from third parties through the demo we will have."*

We described a series of possible analyses, but let's focus on two of them in a sketching session.

- The features are okay, but the game is not fun.

- The game is fun but very difficult to play.

The Features Are Okay, but the Game Is Not Fun

The game is simple and focuses on movement, demanding attention regarding the position, so the players can have a new experience in a 2D game.

You learned from the feedback that the playability and mechanics work well, but the game is not fun, so the players aren't overly interested in the game and won't promote it. How can you make the experience more fun so that players have fun and will promote your game?

ACTION ITEM

Title: Improving the game experience.

Description: The features of the game are okay; however, the game experience is not fun, and it's necessary to brainstorm solutions.

Context: Based on the learnings you received via the test feedback, the game is not interesting to play, although it's working very well.

Analysis: The tests on demos showed you that, in spite of the good playability, it's necessary to improve the game experience, adding aspects that provide more fun.

First Ideation

The goal here is to ideate so that the game becomes more fun. By reading an action item, you can get more information about what happened. Let's suppose that the game doesn't present enough difficulty. Thus, some of the possible ideas can involve including new elements. Some suggestions may be enemies, collectibles, weather, powers, or any other obstacle.

The Game Is Fun But Very Difficult to Play

The game is a 2D platform that brings new playability experiences. It aims to allow players to experience the entertainment of a platform, but with an extra touch of genius.

Note that the game mechanics are not adjusted to the scenery environment, making it impossible for the player to overcome the obstacles. How can you solve this issue so the game becomes effectively playable?

ACTION ITEMS

Title: Improving movement mechanics.

Description: It's necessary to make the game mechanics more real or improve them so the game experience is better.

Context: Based on the knowledge you gained via the test feedback, you noticed that, although they were having fun, the players had lots of difficulties in overcoming obstacles and getting used to the mechanics.

Analysis: Improving the game mechanics will make the playability experience and the narrative complement each other better.

Second Ideation

The ideation at this point aims to identify what the game difficulty is and to propose solutions. The difficulties can be poorly implemented features, irregular jumps, lack of predictability about movements, and much more.

Let's suppose that the jump implementation is irregular, making it difficult to jump from one platform to another and hindering the process of eliminating enemies. Some suggestions might be to rethink the jump, verify whether the implementation can achieve the desired goals, verify whether the jump design matches the level design, verify whether the level matches the different game metrics, and much more.

Rethink the Limitations on Game Development

In general, you have verified several limitations in the first stages of game development; however, many times, it's necessary to rethink the limitations. Here are some ideas:

- *Which platform is the most important now?*[1] PC? PlayStation 4? Xbox One? Android? iOS? You should know which ones you are implementing for, which one is easiest, what difficulties the current platform brings you, and other obstacles that might come up. Tip: In general, the PC is the easiest platform to develop and has the least issues on available resources.

- *Should you avoid something?* What kind of player are you looking to reach? For instance, should you avoid using lots of buttons for young children, or should you avoid using simple commands in the case of mobile platforms? Is the MVP about reaching all kinds of players, or should you focus on a single type?

- *How are inputs and outputs going to happen?* Are you using joysticks, a mouse, and Oculus Rift, or will you use only the keyboard?

- *Are the mechanics easily adjustable?* Were they correctly implemented, and are they easily improved in case you need them in the next MVPs?

---

[1] In the Nintendo vs Sega era, the amount of exclusive games was huge and porting meant a lot of work. In the Xbox 360 vs PS3 era, the cell processor gave developers way more headaches than the Microsoft Xbox. This would generally lead to programming for Xbox in PC then, later, porting it to PS3.

- *Can you improve the scripts without breaking the game's experience?* The code needs to be refactorable and loosely coupled so that future changes don't break the code and the game's overall experience.

It is at this point that you are closing a Lean development loop. It's time to rethink your ideas, rethink the hypotheses, iterate to fix the design, and improve the build. You have reached the point where you can really say that you generated learning, as you propose solutions to the problems encountered, share these problems and their solutions with the collective, and plan the next moments.

Converting Ideas into Epics and Stories

Now that you have metrics for your hypotheses, feedback, analysis of your results, and ideas for improving the game, you come to the part that every developer complains about—the "Jira," that is, the board (Kanban, Scrum, or any other possibility) that will manage, organize, and prioritize the tasks. This section focuses specifically on my way of doing things and how that reflects on my experiences in productions, big and small.

To me, action items are pretty much the equivalent of *epics*, a more abstract concept of a large set of actions with deep analysis and more general context. I separate related epics into initiatives, which are the realization of a common goal. Action items are often so complex that they end up becoming initiatives; and, in large projects, these initiatives end up becoming temporary teams that focus on resolving the related epics.

At the beginning of a project, epics accumulate and are prioritized in different sequences or initiatives; however, not all epics need deep drilling or task sequencing right away. For the epics on which you will start work immediately, focus on discussing with all the stakeholders (PO, UX, technical director, other teams, technical leaders, and production managers) to obtain an in-depth context, all the necessary analyses, and a technical context of what you are going to develop. That way, the team lead, often with the entire team involved in the initiative, can write the stories that you are going to work on—the user stories.

A *story* is a more granular concept than an epic. It represents a piece of something that needs to be developed to achieve the feature represented in the epic. Stories do not necessarily represent the task to be developed itself—these are usually called *tasks*, and I differentiate them by how long they will take, the number of disciplines involved, and how well defined they are. I often create stories that contain some tasks, especially things that can be parallelized, like investigations or feature development in libraries and in the game. How do you differentiate a task from a story?

- If the work to be done is multidisciplinary or not very specific to a discipline (they might need to collaborate), a *story* is probably more suitable. Another case might be when the work is not clear and well defined. However, that could be a *spike*. On the other hand, if the team knows exactly what to do, where to do something, or what the expected granular result should be, a *task* can be a good solution.

- *Tasks* are best for generating work complexity estimates, as I focus on them as well-defined, granular tasks. My teams manage to accomplish several tasks per week or even per day, but stories are hardly done in less than a week, usually generating more work to be done.

- *Spikes* are another interesting concept, when you want to timebox a job to investigate a subject, it's called a spike. It can have as a deliverable a code submission or even a set of tasks to develop the work.

- Another big difference is the disciplines involved, as I
  mentioned in the first item. In a game, many disciplines
  can be involved in a single feature, such as UX,
  programming, art, gameplay, release, and marketing.
  My team focuses on the first three (UX, programming,
  and art) and, when I create a story, the UX concept is
  much broader and covers the entire feature, in addition
  to having a less technical description. But when I create
  a task, I narrow down the UX concept in which the
  developers or artists should work. Note that tasks are
  generally restricted to artists or developers.

One last tip in this regard is how to write stories and tasks. I usually
write them like this:

STORIES/TASK EXAMPLE

As a **[user persona II technical discipline]**

I want **[user's objective with the work]**.

Currently, we can do **[partial state of the feature II complete state]**

So we need to implement **[missing feature concept]**

Add technical limitations or current technical knowledge to tasks**:**

An example of this is as follows:

As a game designer,

*I want to be able to create maps based on my art in an auto-
mated way.*

*Currently, it is possible to create the maps manually, adding
element by element.*

So we need to implement a 2D digital art-reading tool that converts to 3D.

Considering the limitations that orthographic 2D art has and that it is possible to make adjustments to the final result, add all the expected images and UX details.

Summary

This chapter was short but was a key component of the Lean cycle. You have to think about everything you have done so far, so you can generate new ideas and evolve the previous ideas to continue developing the game in the following iterations. The chapter also reviewed the different concepts of workflow with epics, initiatives, stories, and tasks.

CHAPTER 13

Consolidating Knowledge Before Expanding

If you recall, the book began by covering preconceptions in the game industry regarding Lean and Agile methodologies. This chapter reviews and discusses each of those points:

1. Test automation in games is much more complex than in other software industries.

2. The visuals and art cannot be tested automatically.

3. Open betas and demos for kids to test the game are much cheaper.

4. The current business model in the industry is crazy and based on off-the-shelf games.

5. "I don't like Scrum," as if Scrum were the absolute answer to Agile methodologies.

6. Game sequences are not iterations.

7. Art cannot be iterated—and games are art.

© Julia Naomi Rosenfield Boeira 2024
J. N. Rosenfield Boeira, *Lean Game Development*,
https://doi.org/10.1007/978-1-4842-9843-5_13

8. Games are designed so that users play longer, not to save the users time.

9. It is not possible to create an automated testing pyramid for games.

10. From a production standpoint, continuous delivery is not attractive for games.

Automated Testing

Based on automated testing, here are my replies to the statements made in Items 1, 2, 3, 9:

- Test automation may be more complex in gaming than other fields, but it is certainly as or more valuable.

- I wrote an entire book (in Portuguese) about automated testing for games, *TDD para Games*, published by Casa do Code.

- Gameplay tests and tests to identify errors in images, as well as how close an image is to the ideal, are fundamental resources for games. With Bevy's new capture game screen system, you can easily verify game states.

- Using kids to test games, even if it generates some degree of satisfaction, is morally wrong and can greatly affect the reception of a game. Besides that, they are far from professionals. As mentioned previously, the only exception is when they are your target audience and their parents are involved in the process.

Test automation in the software industry is often represented by a test pyramid, in which the base is unit testing and the top of the pyramid is end-to-end testing, passing through smoke, integration, functional, and contract testing. When we say that testing games is more complex, we usually refer to specific parts, like gameplay, because that's the part the industry sees as automated testing, a type of testing that replaces the "tester person" and automates their work. This type of testing is important, but it hardly improves the quality of the developed product, as it focuses more on final results. Many bugs can only be captured by more granular testing.

In recent years, the games industry seems to have realized this fact and many engines have started to support test systems that allow the execution of unit tests, integration tests, and even functional tests. Unfortunately, these engines and supported systems still struggle with the idea that testing first or writing tests for code that has been written is a waste of time, as more time is spent writing test code than algorithms. Fortunately, I can speak from my own experience that teams that have a good test pyramid deliver better quality software, with less risk and fewer defects. This optimizes production time and earnings. In my experience managing teams, those who were more rigorous about testing found far fewer defects and integration issues than those who only wrote production code.

It's easy to say, but difficult to execute, and that's why I've been writing and publishing material on how to do software development using the test pyramid and TDD, such as *TDD for Games*. I've also seen many libraries that allow visual tests for precision and approximation, being able to set minimum similarity thresholds or variance points, since the randomness factor is fundamental to games. Speaking of randomness, using test pyramids makes the quality of written software better, as tests don't work very well with coupling and tend to favor composition over complex hierarchies.

Finally, I want to point out that using children to test games can cause them anxiety, since the game mechanics can be poorly defined and the tasks can be unattainable. In addition, game trials often require many hours of play and small fees are often offered, which can cause legal issues regarding the payment of children for their work. In this sense, functional and end-to-end testing can identify recurring failures or mechanical issues with each change.

Agility

This section refers to Items 4, 5, and 6 of the list presented at the beginning of this chapter. Agile is not restricted to Scrum, which is just one among several other methodologies. Furthermore, they are all based on an original manifesto, and the main (but not only) keywords in Agile and Lean methodologies are:

- **Kanban**: This is a project scope and status visualization tool that allows flexibility and predictability. Kanban often requires on-demand planning meetings or a person responsible for planning and organizing tasks. It is usually defined on a board that contains at least three columns for tasks states: To Do, Doing, and Done.

- **Scrum**: This is not very different from Kanban, but it defines its work cycles in *sprints* and therefore introduces a series of meetings associated with the start and end of each sprint. Many teams define sprints as rigid periods of something like two weeks, but more traditionally, sprints should be equivalent to the planned cycle and not be interfered with by future cycles. Many teams that use Kanban inherit some meeting cycles from Scrum.

- **eXtreme programming**: In my opinion, this is one key methodology among all Agile methodologies. XP is associated with development practices. It focuses on continual intervals of development and iteration over the results. In addition, it proposes a series of techniques that I consider fundamental, such as small releases, pair programming, TDD, continuous delivery, code refactoring, sense of collective code ownership, and code development patterns.

- **Crystal**: This is a family of frameworks that focus primarily on people and their interactions.

- **Lean**: This is usually grouped with Agile methodologies due to their similar values, but it is something completely different. It focuses on eliminating waste, on quality as an integral part of the project, on sharing knowledge, on delivering fast and maximizing learning for each delivery—that is, on optimizing the whole development process.

Taking any of these methodologies as silver bullets can generate more discomfort and disorganization, as many of them require a cultural change in the company, especially from the leader's perspective. One of the main examples of this is understanding what a game MVP is, what a finished game is, what can be extended from this MVP/finished game, as well as continuously collecting feedback, acting on the collected feedback, and creating development and learning cycles—but, more than that, not letting these learnings go to waste in the next releases.

Also, it is worth mentioning that Scrum is very widespread and used in the vast majority of serious studios, from indies to AAA. This aversion exists in a few small indie studios and some old school large studios, which end up making a lot of noise. One of the main reasons for this aversion may be pure ignorance on the topic, ignorance of the tools that can be used, and ignorance on how to apply these tools. Unfortunately, it is very easy to find articles relating an aversion to Agile methodologies and game development because of this.

Art and Iterations

This session refers to Item 7 on the list. I will summarize it with an image of Jeff Patton and what I think is the symbol image of this book. See Figures 13-1 and 13-2.

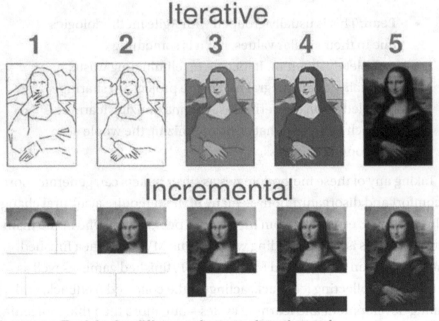

Outcome: Explain the difference between iterative and incremental and how that relates to User Story

Credit: Jeff Patton

Figure 13-1. *Agile methods applied to art. Source: Jeff Patton*

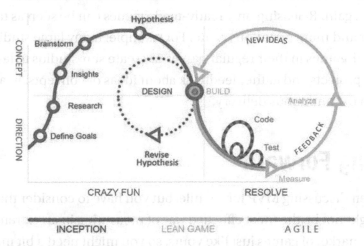

Figure 13-2. *Example of game analytics*

Saving Time

Saving time, as mentioned in Item 8, is not a gaming goal. However, ensuring that the users don't waste their gaming time learning mechanics, adjusting settings, understanding dialogues, or identifying what to do for a given action is certainly a goal. These topics lead to significant improvements in the gaming experience.

Continuous Delivery

To believe that continuous delivery (Items 4 and 10) is not a viable model for games is certainly a misconception. I don't know of any major game company that doesn't have some kind of game delivery phase sequence—a series of events where the game is revisited. These sequences are definitely planning game deliveries. However, they are often not made public to collect feedback, and therefore a lot of resources are wasted with no real knowledge gain. Releasing only ready-made games can be seen as taking the longer and more circuitous route. For example, many large studios can create mini-games in their regular games or create sub-studios to launch small test projects and gather feedback about ideas or concepts, in a model more akin to continuous delivery.

Pushing Forward

I have been discussing MVP for a while, but you have to consider that MVPs might not be the most effective way of measuring in an extremely saturated market of games just like yours, so you might need a bit more. This is where the Minimum Lovable Product, or game, comes into play.

Note   MVPs market your product fast and at a low cost. However, many consumers are wanting a WOW in the games they play.[1]

This wow MVP might mean that you need to spend a little more time developing your game concept so you achieve a minimum lovable experience.

---

[1] https://productschool.com/blog/product-strategy/
minimum-lovable-product

What Is a Minimum Lovable Game?

The MLG, or minimum lovable game,[2] is similar to the MVP in the sense that it is the minimum game that you have to deliver to prove an idea, get feedback, and iterate over it. However, the MLG focuses more on a true vertical cut of the game idea and experience, giving more emphasis to the game design and experience.

An MLG doesn't invalidate an MVP and it can still use MVPs as resources and process stages. However, the key points are as follows:[3]

- **Goal**: MVPs focus on collecting feedback to validate or refute an idea and carefully plan the development strategy. On the other hand, MLGs target the early adopters to hype the game.

- **Time and cost**: MVPs are easy and quick to develop and validate. MLGs are riskier and take longer to develop, with probably more people engaged.

- **Design and experience**: MVPs are more about the game features and mechanics, while MLGs are focused on the game design and game experience. The MLG might require a bunch of MVPs, prototypes, and iterations to get it ready to be loved.

- **Relationship with users**: MVPs focus on getting user feedback to improve the game, while MLGs focus on making targeted early adopters hype the game, ideally creating a word-of-mouth effect.

---

[2] https://medium.com/riot-games-ux-design/the-ux-behind-theunlock-at-riot-games-part-1-97ec6dd189be

[3] https://agilie.com/blog/minimum-lovable-product-what-a-mlp-is-and-how-to-create-one

Benefits of MLGs

The MLG benefits from the MVPs and minimum marketable products by combining and utilizing them and giving them an extra twist. This twist is *increased competitiveness*. This is due to the fact that lovable games have a better chance to appeal to players and make them loyal, increasing the game's competitiveness.

Early branding is another benefit of MLG. You might still have a lot of ideas to include in your game with iterations and delivery sequences. However, an MLG allows you to deliver an awesome result that engages the audience right from the start. This is also a low time to market strategy when comparing it with fully featured games. One example of this can be seasons that include new players, maps, guns, and stories in FPS games.

Lastly, an MLG allows you to stay Lean and Agile, while focusing on delivering the minimum. *Minimum* is a keyword here, as it allows you to keep MVP processes but deliver something extra. You could say that the *Archero* game delivered something like this, because features came as people progressed and engaged with the game.

Summary

This chapter revisited the core complaints people have about Lean and Agile methodologies. However, this time, I used the information in this book to quickly review why these complaints can be dismissed and how to overcome them. The main topics discussed were as follows:

- Automated testing

- Agility

- Art and iterations

- Saving time

- Continuous delivery

- Minimum lovable games

CHAPTER 14

More About Games

How do you differentiate and classify everything we usually call games?

There could be hundreds of categories that come to mind when you think about games, including serious games, gamification, adver-games, and many others. A very simple way to see these differences, in my opinion, is in Table 14-1.

Table 14-1. *Differences Between the Things We Call Games (The X Represents a Requirement.)*

Game Class	Game Thinking	Game Elements	Virtual World	Gameplay	Not Purposeful
Playful Games	x				
Gamification	x	x			
Adver-games		x	x		
Simulations	x	x	x		
Serious Games	x	x	x	x	
Digital Games	x	x	x	x	x

Figure 14-1 shows, according to Andrzej Marczewski in *Even Ninja Monkeys Like to Play* (2015), a classification of game types.

© Julia Naomi Rosenfield Boeira 2024
J. N. Rosenfield Boeira, *Lean Game Development*,
https://doi.org/10.1007/978-1-4842-9843-5_14

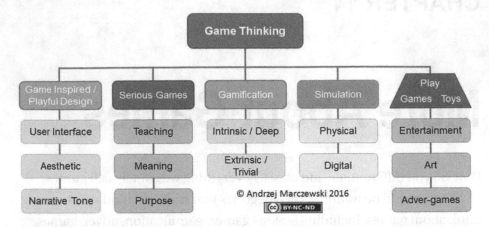

Figure 14-1. *Classification of game types. Source: Marczewski, 2015.*

Here's a brief explanation of each of the categories in Figure 14-1—and a few more:

- **Playful games**: Games that revolve around the workings and thinking of games, but do not have strongly attributed game elements. It turns out that the interface resembles a game.

- **Gamification**: Revolves around the concept of creating something that *feels like a game*. It consists of turning an idea into something playable and introducing game elements.

- **Serious games**: Complete games created for reasons other than pure entertainment. Usually they challenge you to empathize with some other group.

- **Games for learning/teaching**: Games created with the intention of helping people learn or teaching something specific while playing a real game.

- **Meaningful games**: Games that convey meaningful messages to the players, such as teaching some aspect of conflict, the reality of some social groups, and much more. Frequently associated with serious games.

- **Purposeful games**: Games that return some kind of real result. This can encompass meaningful games, learning games, and serious games.

- **Simulation/sandbox**: A virtual representation of some real aspect. It doesn't necessarily require gameplay and usually has some purpose, often military or evolutionary.

- **Entertaining games**: It's difficult to define the concept, but as you have seen, the class is wide. Recall that entertainment games can belong to several categories, including those mentioned previously. Many call pure entertainment and art games *play games*, which can be confusing with *playful games*. They are an art form and often referred to as digitally interactive films or storytelling.

- **Mixed reality and metaverse**: Games that include virtual reality and augmented reality. In some cases, such as in the metaverse, they are no longer just games and become technology-based entertainment experiences. Apple Vision Pro and Microsoft Hololens create a whole new gaming experience.

Book Recap

From this point on, the book becomes more programming/engineering technical, so I want to stop here and quickly recap the topics.

You have learned how to use different techniques, such as inceptions, MVPs (MVG and prototypes), hypotheses, feedback, metrics analysis, TDD, continuous integration, and design and build planning for game development. The goal is to avoid reinventing the wheel every time a game is developed. This is achieved by optimizing the whole and defining clear objectives and a vision of what must be delivered on each delivery.

These techniques were discussed especially for digital games with the objective of entertainment, but they can be applied to any type of software that uses *game thinking*. So, when it comes to developing your next game (or software product), think about how much it can contribute to the community—rather than how to do it.

The last two chapters discuss how to configure the Unity engine to execute automated testing for a character controller, run those tests in a CI, and try different testing solutions.

Note   All future updated solutions and ideas can be found on my GitHub at `https://github.com/naomijub`.

CHAPTER 15

Automated Testing with Unity

This chapter explains how to create a basic character controller in Unity by TDD and set up GitHub Actions to work as the CI/CD platform. The code can be found at `https://github.com/naomijub/FPSwithTDD`, while the playable demo can be found at `https://naomijub.github.io/FPSwithTDD/`.

For game development frameworks like Monogame, GGEZ, Raylib, Pygame, LibGDX, and Phaser, which behave like packages (libraries, crates, or whatever you call them), it is fairly easy to develop games and get good test coverage. Sadly, most games developed with these frameworks are poorly tested or not tested at all. Besides famous game development frameworks, there are a few game engines that allow you to perform some level of testing, especially when you use the language-native testing resources, such as Panda3D, Amethyst, AppGameKit, and jMonkey. However, when it comes to the big engines in the market like Unity, Unreal, and CryEngine, the reality is not that simple. Fortunately, they have been putting great effort into making games testable and, in my opinion, Unity is in a more advanced stage.

J. N. Rosenfield Boeira, *Lean Game Development*,
https://doi.org/10.1007/978-1-4842-9843-5_15

I first heard of automated testing via Unity a few years back when they released their package called *Unity Test Tools.*[1] This package was deprecated and later included in the current *Unity Test Runner,* which is now incorporated into the engine. Test runners are basically test executors and, in the case of Unity, it's a test executor that can run specific Unity-related tests. Around the same time I saw a few talks from Tomek Paszek where he expressed that one of the motivations behind the Unity Test Tools package was the fact that some parts of Unity were being developed with unit testing, but there was no testing resource for the games themselves.

Currently, it is fairly easy to find resources about testing and game development, and there is even an article written by Sophia Clarke called "Testing Test Driven Development with Unity,"[2] where she explores the viability of developing a game with TDD in Unity. Also, I highly recommend reading the N-Unit[3] C# test package documentation, as it is the default test package for Unity. In the next section, you start the test environment setup and write some very simple tests.

Configuring Unity Test Environment

The first thing you need to do is download the latest Unity version. This book was written using Unity 2020.3.16f1 LTS, so the test setup is supposed to be usable in a few later versions, as well as versions 2018 and 2019. With the Unity Hub downloaded, log in and activate your license. Then choose version 2020.3.16f1 LTS and download it.

Unity has two test annotations, [Test] and [UnityTest]. The difference between them is that [UnityTest] can execute in Play Mode and make assertions over actions and events in Play Mode, whereas

---

[1] https://github.com/spe3d/unitytesttools
[2] https://blog.unity.com/technology/testing-test-driven-development-with-the-unity-test-runner
[3] https://docs.nunit.org/

[Test] executes only over functions that are independent from Play Mode, namely Edit Mode. The following step-by-step instructions may seem trivial, but they might be altered from version to version, so it is important to have them written down. That way, at least for the 2020 LTS version, anyone can do it.

Here are the step-by-step instructions for configuring automated testing in Unity:

1. Download Unity Hub at https://store.unity. com/pt/download.

2. Log in and activate your license in Preferences.

3. Download Unity version 2020.3.16f1 LTS, or the latest compatible version.

4. Click New to create a new project.

5. Choose the 3D template and a project name.

6. To find the test runner, go to Window ➤ General ➤ Test Runner. Figure 15-1 shows the Test Runner window.

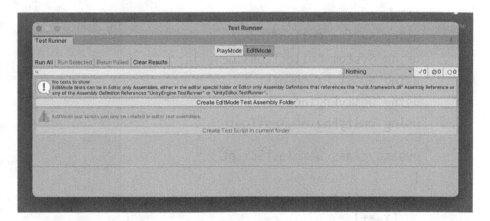

Figure 15-1. *Unity Test Runner window*

At first, the Test Runner will be empty, as no test has been configured. Follow these steps next:

1. To create a test assembly folder, click the Create EditMode Test Assembly folder and then a folder called Tests will be created.

2. If you open the test assembly file inside the Tests folder, you will see a bunch of preselected configurations. Be sure to check the desired test platforms in the Platforms field.

3. Now you need to create a demo test. To do that, click Create Test Script in the Current Folder. I named my new test script DemoTestScript. If you open the test script, you will see that the two testing frameworks are being used—NUnit.Framework for using [Test] and Assert as well as UnityEngine.TestTools for using [UnityTest]. UnityTest should have a return type of IEnumerator and you can use yield return null to skip one frame.

```
```
using System.Collections;
using System.Collections.Generic;
using NUnit.Framework;
using UnityEngine;
using UnityEngine.TestTools;

public class DemoTestScript
{
    // A Test behaves as an ordinary method
    [Test]
    public void DemoTestScriptSimplePasses()
```
```

```
{
    // Use the Assert class to test conditions
}

// A UnityTest behaves like a coroutine in Play
    Mode. In Edit Mode you can use
// `yield return null;` to skip a frame.
[UnityTest]
public IEnumerator
DemoTestScriptWithEnumeratorPasses()
{
    // Use the Assert class to test conditions.
    // Use yield to skip a frame.
    yield return null;
}
}
```

4.   To run the tests, go to the Test Runner and click Run
     All. Figure 15-2 shows the test execution.

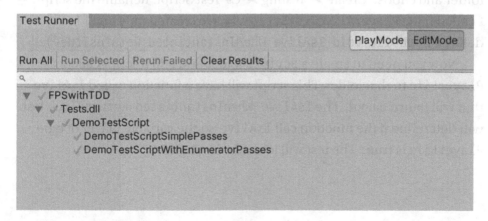

Figure 15-2. *Edit Mode test execution*

5. There is another annotation that may be interesting to know about. [UnityPlatform] helps you determine the target (or excluded) platform to execute the tests. To define a target platform, let's say Windows, you define it as [UnityPlatform(RuntimePlatform. WindowsEditor)]. To exclude the Windows platform, you can use [UnityPlatform(exclude = new[] {RuntimePlatform.WindowsEditor })].

6. Finally, it is important to know that if you want to test logs, you can use the Unity assertion for logs as follows: LogAssert.Expect(LogType.Log, "Log message").

Writing Your First Test

The first test that you will write determines if your player is alive. To create this test, you need to create a new test script. To do that, go to the Tests folder and choose Create ➤ Testing ➤ C# Test Script. Rename the script; I called mine PlayerAliveTestScript. I have created only one [Test] defined by public void IsAlive_WhenInstantiated_ReturnsTrue().

Now you need to create a Scripts folder and add a script called PlayerLife to that folder. This script will have a function called IsAlive that will return a bool. The IsAlive_WhenInstantiated_ReturnsTrue test will determine if the function call IsAlive on the variable player of type PlayerLife is true. The test will look like Listing 15-1.

Listing 15-1. Initial Test Setup

```
[Test]
public void IsAlive_WhenInstantiated_ReturnsTrue()
{
    var player = new PlayerLife();
    Assert.AreEqual(true, player.IsAlive());
}
```

You need to make this test compile by creating the function called IsAlive in the PlayerLife script (see Listing 15-2). Be aware that if your script inherits from MonoBehaviour you should not use the new PlayerLife() constructor declaration. It works with this warning "You are trying to create a MonoBehaviour using the new keyword. This is not allowed. MonoBehaviours can only be added using AddComponent(). Alternatively, your script can inherit from ScriptableObject or no base class at all."

Listing 15-2. Implementation of the IsAlive Function to the Compile Test

```
using System.Collections;
using System.Collections.Generic;
using UnityEngine;

public class PlayerLife : MonoBehaviour
{
    public bool IsAlive() {
        return false;
    }
}
```

However, if you try to execute the test runner, you will get a message saying "Assets/Tests/PlayerAliveTestScript.cs(12,26): error CS0246: The type or namespace name 'PlayerLife' could not be found (are you missing a using directive or an assembly reference?)".

This compilation error is telling you that, to associate the scripts with the tests, you need an *assembly reference*. To solve this problem, you need to right-click the Scripts folder and choose Create ➤ Assembly Definition. I named my scripts assembly definition <Something>ScriptsDefinition. With this done, you can go to the Tests folder assembly definition and create a new Assembly Definition Reference by clicking the + button. Then drag and drop the assembly definition from the scripts folder into the Missing Reference field. See Figure 15-3.

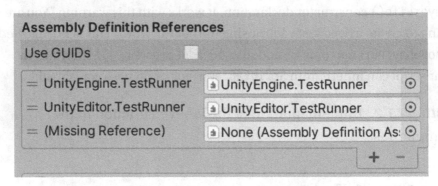

Figure 15-3. *Missing assembly reference window*

To make this test pass, you can, for now, make it return true and have the test pass. The last step is to fix the warning "You are trying to create a MonoBehaviour using the 'new' keyword...". To do that, you need to define a [SetUp] annotation that creates a GameObject and adds the PlayerLife component to it. With this change, you can use GetComponent<PlayerLife>() instead of declaring a new PlayerLife() every time you need to access the MonoBehaviour. See Listings 15-3 and 15-4.

Listing 15-3. Refactoring Test Setup

```
```

using System.Collections;
using System.Collections.Generic;
using NUnit.Framework;
using UnityEngine;
using UnityEngine.TestTools;

public class PlayerAliveTestScript
{
    GameObject go;

    [SetUp]
    public void SetUp() {
        go = new GameObject("test");
        go.AddComponent<PlayerLife>();
    }

    [Test]
    public void IsAlive_WhenInstantiated_ReturnsTrue()
    {
        PlayerLife player = go.GetComponent<PlayerLife>();

        Assert.AreEqual(true,player.IsAlive());
    }
}
```
```

Listing 15-4. IsAlive Passes the Test

```
```

using System.Collections;
using System.Collections.Generic;
using UnityEngine;
```
```

```
public class PlayerLife : MonoBehaviour
{
    public bool IsAlive() {
        return true;
    }
}
```

Next, you need to configure your CI with GitHub Actions, so the development process has every integration verified.

CI for Unity

I am of the opinion that every modern software project should have a CI/CD pipeline associated with it, and Unity is no exception. There are a few options for configuring a CI for Unity, but the most obvious one is Unity Cloud Build.[4] It is Unity's native CI tool, and it is very well documented. However, it may not be the perfect tool for your project and it works better as a continuous builder-only tool than a CI/CD tool. The other obvious choice is to use some kind of CI like GitHub Actions, GitLab CI, Travis-CI, Game.CI, or CircleCI. Unfortunately, I have had a lot of problems configuring Unity's CI with Travis-CI and I do not recommend it. Even though it did work at some point, it has to be continuously fixed for future changes. Most of my projects are on GitHub, so I usually choose GitHub Actions as my CI. The best way to create a Unity GitHub Actions is with the newly created Game.CI, which is a rebrand of Unity Actions, combined with Unity Builder for the build step.

---

[4]https://docs.unity.com/devops/en/manual/unity-build-automation

Dockerizing Unity

A very important feature for CIs is the ability to dockerize their programs. In Unity, that can be done with Game-ci/docker. These are specialized Unity Docker images for CI and command-line tools, which are named unity-ci/editor.[5] You choose your unity version. The only problem with this, so far, is the limited IL2CPP support (Ubuntu Only) and versions newer than 2019. You can find your Unity version in Unity Hub, as shown in Figure 15-4.

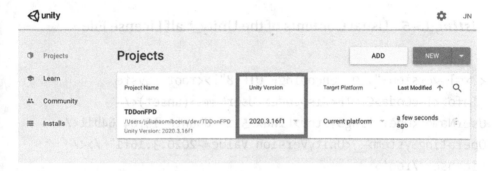

Figure 15-4.   *Unity version in Unity Hub*

To execute this Docker image, you can run the `docker run -it unityci/editor:ubuntu-2020.3.16f1-mac-mono-0` command, which means you want to run a Docker container (`unityci/editor`) in interactive mode (`-it`) with the `ubuntu-2020.3.16f1-mac-mono-0` tag. The Unity editor will be located at `/opt/unity/Editor` as Unity.

Now you need to create the activation file. To do that, change your directory to the `Editors` directory by executing `cd /opt/unity/Editor` and run the `./Unity -quit -batchmode -nographics -lgFile -createManualActivationFile` command. You will see a message saying the manual activation license file was saved.

---

[5] `https://hub.docker.com/r/unityci/editor`

The -quit flag tells Unity it needs to quit after executing these commands, the -batchmode means it is only going to run on the command line, -nographics means no graphic device is going to be initialized, -logFile outputs the log to the console, and -createManualActivationFile generates a file that allows you to create a license for the Docker. You can see the file by executing ls. It will be named Unity_v2020.3.16f1.alf. To get the alf file content, you can execute cat Unity_v2020.3.16f1.alf and copy its content (from <?xml...> to the contents shown in Listing 15-5).

Listing 15-5. Usual Contents of the Unity_*.alf License File

```
<?xml version="1.0" encoding="UTF-8"?><root><Syste
mInfo><IsoCode>C.UTF</IsoCode><UserName>(unset)</
UserName><OperatingSystem>Linux 5.10 Ubuntu 18.04 64bit</
OperatingSystem>__<UnityVersion Value="2020.3.16f1" /></
License></root>
```

Save this file on your machine as an alf file and go to Unity's activation page[6] to get your license file. Download the Unity*.ulf license file. Then send the file to your Docker container by executing docker cp ./Unity_ v2020.x.ulf 1c25b08a74dd:/opt/unity/Editor, which means copy a file from a file location in the host to container_id 1c25... at path /opt/unity/ Editor. The container ID can be found by using docker ps, and you can activate it by executing ./Unity -batchmode -manualLicenseFile Unity_ v2020.x.ulf -logfile. Now you can run any game command with /Unity as long as your container has an associated Dockerfile to build the container with the necessary project files. The game commands that you will run inside the container are equal to the ones you will execute in GitHub Actions.

---

[6]https://license.unity3d.com/manual

Configuring GitHub

There are not a lot of secrets to working with Git and Unity. One important thing is to make sure that you have an up-to-date .gitignore file and you are forcing your .meta files to be in text mode. To generate an up-to-date .gitignore file, I recommend checking www.toptal.com/developers/gitignore/api/unity. Just take care when ignoring [Oo]bj and [Bb]uild because some objects and folders use those names and can be ignored.

Another important issue in game development is file locking, which means that only one person can edit a file at a time. This is because Git cannot resolve merge conflicts for blob files with its standard tools. Sound effects, 3D objects, sprite sheets, fonts, tiles, and binaries in general need locking. Prefabs and even meta files can cause huge merging conflicts if they are not locked. The first recommendation is to have your locked files concentrated in one or a few folders that don't have code or not frequently edited code.

Two important concepts to explore related to locking are partial clones and sparse checkouts. *Partial clones* allow you to avoid downloading large binary folders. You can clone them whenever you need them in a just-in-time manner, discarding the binary objects history. This will help you work only with the latest binaries. A partial clone that removes binaries (blobs) is defined as a clone with a filter tag defining blobs to none, git clone --filter=blobs:none, which will download the blob's metadata but not the file content itself. The *sparse flag*, --sparse, can be used to clone only the files in the root directory and can be used to avoid downloading the blob folders in less complex projects. The whole command is git clone --filter=blob:none --sparse git@git.path.git. To retrieve the missing folders without caring about their history, you can use the sparse checkout command with the path to the folder/file, such as git sparse-checkout add /path/to/folder/or/file.

With these techniques, you can now learn about file locking. File locking means that nobody can write to that file unless they explicitly ask. You can lock a file by using the git-lfs file-locking feature. This doesn't mean you need to store the files in git-lfs, you just use its locking feature. To use git-lfs, be sure you have lfs installed on your machine and CI and then install it in your project with git lfs install.

To use the git-lfs locking feature, use a file called .gitattributes, which is a collection of file patterns and attributes, something like **/*. png lockable, which sets the attribute lockable to all PNG files in path **/*. To lock a file for local development, you can type git lfs lock / path/to/file. You should receive a message saying Locked /path/to/ file. This will lock the file in all branches. To unlock it, add the changes, commit them and push, and then run git lfs unlock /path/to/file. A message saying Unlocked /path/to/lock will appear.

Configuring GitHub Actions

You have already generated a license, and now you need to generate a .github/workflow that activates that license. The first step is to go to your repository in GitHub and click Actions. Since Unity doesn't have a preset workflow, you need to click Set Up a Workflow Yourself, which will automatically be called main.yml. See Listing 15-6.

Listing 15-6. Basic GitHub Actions Example

```
```
name: CI

on:
 push:
   branches: [main]
 pull_request:
   branches: [main]
 workflow_dispatch:
```

188
```

```
jobs:
 build:
   runs-on: ubuntu-latest
   steps:
     - uses: actions/checkout@v2
     - name: Run a one-line script
       run: echo Hello, world!
     - name: Run a multi-line script
       run: |
         echo Add other actions to build,
         echo test, and deploy your project.
```

Now you can create another .yml file named activation.yml at
.github/workflows, which will be responsible for getting Unity's license
file. See Listing 15-7.

Listing 15-7. GitHub Action for Unity License Activation

```
name: Gets Unity license activation file

on: workflow_dispatch

jobs:
 getManualActivationFile:
   name: Gets manual activation file
   runs-on: ubuntu-latest
   steps:
     - uses: actions/checkout@v2
     - uses: game-ci/unity-request-activation-file@v2
       id: getManualLicenseFile
     - uses: actions/upload-artifact@v2
       with:
```

```
    name: Manual Activation File
    path: ${{ steps.getManualLicenseFile.outputs.
    filePath }}
```

The `name` tag is just the name of the action to be executed and `on:`
`workflow_dispatch` means that this will only be executed when you order
it to dispatch. There will be one job named `getManualActivationFile`
running on an Ubuntu machine. This workflow needs to be manually
triggered and it will generate a manual activation file. To do this, choose
Actions ➤ Get Unity License Activation File ➤ Run Workflow. Once it
is done, the file will be available to download at the workflow execution
under the name `Manual Activation File`.

Download the file and unzip it to retrieve the `.alf` file and follow the
same process as you did with Docker to retrieve the `.ulf` file. Go to your
repository Settings, and then in Secrets, copy the `.ulf` file contents and
paste them into a new repository secret called `UNITY_LICENSE`. Figures 15-5
to 15-7 demonstrate this process.

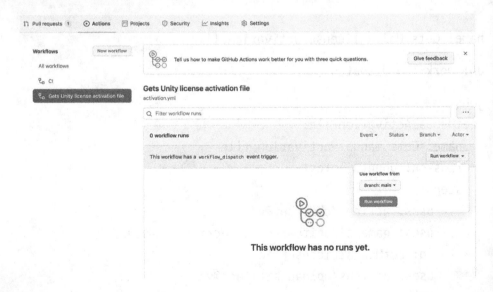

Figure 15-5. *Execute the activate license workflow*

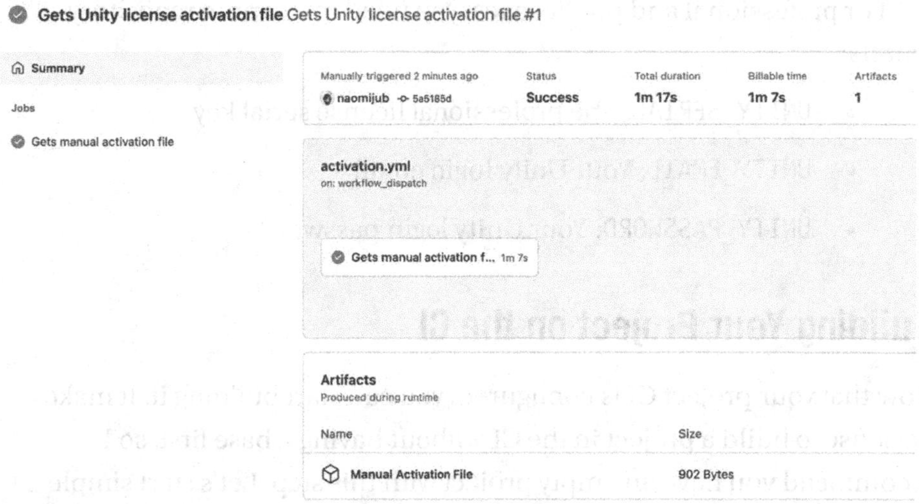

✅ **Gets Unity license activation file** Gets Unity license activation file #1

🏠 Summary					
Jobs	Manually triggered 2 minutes ago	Status	Total duration	Billable time	Artifacts
✅ Gets manual activation file	🔵 naomijub -○- 5a5185d	**Success**	**1m 17s**	**1m 7s**	**1**

activation.yml
on: workflow_dispatch

✅ Gets manual activation f... 1m 7s

Artifacts
Produced during runtime

Name	Size
🗍 Manual Activation File	902 Bytes

Figure 15-6. *Download the activation file*

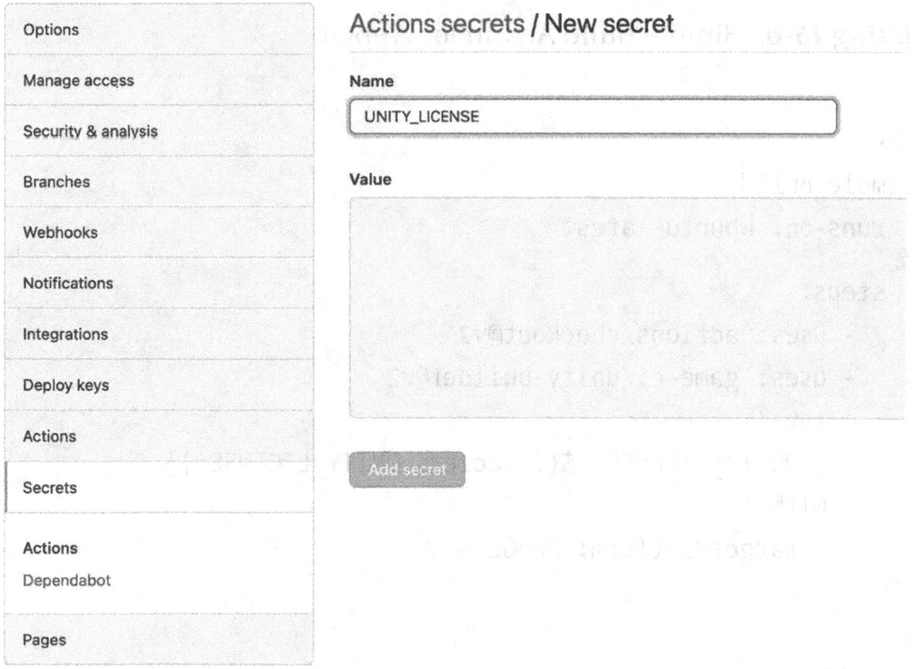

Options	**Actions secrets / New secret**
Manage access	**Name**
Security & analysis	UNITY_LICENSE
Branches	
Webhooks	**Value**
Notifications	
Integrations	
Deploy keys	
Actions	
Secrets	
Actions Dependabot	Add secret
Pages	

Figure 15-7. *Paste the Unity License content in GitHub*

191

For professional and pro licenses, you need three more repository secrets:

- UNITY_SERIAL: The professional license serial key

- UNITY_EMAIL: Your Unity login email

- UNITY_PASSWORD: Your Unity login password

Building Your Project on the CI

Now that your project CI is configured, you can start building it. It makes no sense to build a project in the CI without having a base first, so I recommend you have an empty project with this step. Let's start simple and then expand the build. The minimal build for the CI is under Jobs. Add the simple_build shown in Listing 15-8.

Listing 15-8. Simple Build Action for WebGL

```
```
jobs:
  simple_build:
    runs-on: ubuntu-latest

    steps:
      - uses: actions/checkout@v2
      - uses: game-ci/unity-builder@v2
        env:
          UNITY_LICENSE: ${{ secrets.UNITY_LICENSE }}
        with:
          targetPlatform: WebGL
```
```

This build will basically use your UNITY_LICENSE secret, which is accessed using ${{ variable }} syntax, to build your project and target the WebGL platform. It maybe be useful to store the built artifact. For that you can add a new step after unity-builder@v2 with the configuration shown in Listing 15-9.

Listing 15-9. Build Action Uploads Artifact

```
- uses: actions/upload-artifact@v2
  with:
    name: <Your build name>
    path: build
```

This build takes a while to execute, and there is a simple way to solve this, which is caching the Library folder. If you check the build description, you will see it took a while to execute all the commands associated with the Library folder. To cache it, you can add the code in Listing 15-10.

Listing 15-10. Caching Library Folder

```
- uses: actions/checkout@v2
- uses: actions/cache@v2
  with:
    path: Library
    key: Library-${{ matrix.targetPlatform }}
    restore-keys: Library-
- uses: game-ci/unity-builder@v2
```

Note that the cache step is before the `unity-builder@v2` step and I added a `matrix.targetPlatform` variable, which you will use soon. If you have only one target platform, use only its name. To include multiple platforms, you have to define a strategy before defining the steps. You can do that by defining the `strategy` tag that contains a matrix tag with all platforms. Also, you can generate a different build for every platform by naming the build `name: Build - ${{ matrix.targetPlatform }}`. See Listing 15-11.

Listing 15-11. Action Target Platform Matrix

```
```
build:
  name: Build - ${{ matrix.targetPlatform }}
  runs-on: ubuntu-latest
  strategy:
    fail-fast: false
    matrix:
      targetPlatform:
        - StandaloneOSX
        - StandaloneWindows
        - StandaloneWindows64
        - StandaloneLinux64
        - iOS
        - Android
        - WebGL
  steps: ...
```
```

There are many other build configurations that you can check out on the GameCI/github/builder[7] page, but for now you are going to start testing this game.

Testing Your Project on the CI

Just like unity-builder on CI, unity-test-runner expects some tests to exist. You should create some Unity tests, which are explained in the next chapter. Test runner is not that easy to start small and expand, and there are many nice configurations you can use to ensure you have a minimal adequate test setup. The test job looks like Listing 15-12.

Listing 15-12. Action to Execute Play Mode and Edit Mode Tests

```
```
jobs:
 testAllModes:
   name: Test in ${{ matrix.testMode }}
   runs-on: ubuntu-latest
   strategy:
     fail-fast: false
     matrix:
       testMode:
         - playmode
         - editmode
   steps:
     - uses: actions/checkout@v2
       with:
         lfs: true
     - uses: actions/cache@v2
```

---

[7] https://game.ci/docs/github/builder/
```

```
    with:
      path: Library
      key: Library-${{ matrix.testMode }}
      restore-keys: |
        Library-
  - uses: game-ci/unity-test-runner@v2
    id: tests
    env:
      UNITY_LICENSE: ${{ secrets.UNITY_LICENSE }}
    with:
      testMode: ${{ matrix.testMode }}
      artifactsPath: ${{ matrix.testMode }}-artifacts
      githubToken: ${{ secrets.GITHUB_TOKEN }}
      checkName: ${{ matrix.testMode }} Test Results
  - uses: actions/upload-artifact@v2
    if: always()
    with:
      name: Test results for ${{ matrix.testMode }}
      path: ${{ steps.tests.outputs.artifactsPath }}
 build: ...
```

This job is defined as testAllModes with a name tag that varies
depending on the matrix.testMode. Unity-test-runner has three
possible modes: playmode, which will only execute Play Mode tests,
editmode, which will only execute Edit Mode tests, and all, which will
execute Play Mode and Edit Mode tests. As a quick reference, Edit Mode
tests are unit level tests that don't execute Start, Awake, and Update
functions from Unity's MonoBehaviour, while Play Mode tests execute
those functions, allowing you some control over how many update frames
you want.

The `testModes` are defined in Strategy ➤ Matrix ➤ `testMode`. I have already talked about caching, but you don't actually need the `testMode` variable for this test. When you execute the `unity-test-runner@v2` with `UNITY_LICENSE`, the `with` tag defines the parameters to be used, in which `testMode` is one of the possible test modes, `artifactsPath` is where you want to upload your test artifacts, `checkName` is the name of the artifact, and `githubToken`, which is automatically generated, allows you to access the GitHub status check results for this test. Lastly, you upload the artifacts in the `actions/upload-artifact@v2` step, defining that it will always be uploaded, `if: always()`, under the name `Test results for $testMode` in the path defined in `artifactsPath`.

Improving Execution Time

One thing that is annoying with this CI configuration is that some large Git files take too long to execute. Fortunately, there is a solution for this, which is to cache the large Git file by adding the script in Listing 15-13 after the checkout action, `actions/checkout@v2`.

Listing 15-13. Caching Large Git Files

```
```
- name: Create LFS file list
  run: git lfs ls-files -l | cut -d' ' -f1 | sort > .lfs-
  assets-id
- name: Restore LFS cache
  uses: actions/cache@v2
  id: lfs-cache
  with:
    path: .git/lfs
    key: ${{ runner.os }}-lfs-${{ hashFiles('.lfs-
    assets-id') }}
```
```

```
- name: Git LFS Pull
  run: |
    git lfs pull
    git add .
    git reset --hard
```

At this point, the complete script with names for each step is shown in Listing 15-14.

Listing 15-14. GitHub Actions with Build and Test

```
name: CI

on:
  push:
    branches: [ main ]
  pull_request:
    branches: [ main ]

  workflow_dispatch:

jobs:
  testAllModes:
    name: Test in ${{ matrix.testMode }}
    runs-on: ubuntu-latest
    strategy:
      fail-fast: false
      matrix:
        testMode:
          - playmode
          - editmode
```

```yaml
steps:
  - name: Checkout code
    uses: actions/checkout@v2
    with:
      lfs: true
  - name: Create LFS file list
    run: git lfs ls-files -l | cut -d' ' -f1 | sort > .lfs-
    assets-id
  - name: Restore LFS cache
    uses: actions/cache@v2
    id: lfs-cache
    with:
      path: .git/lfs
      key: ${{ runner.os }}-lfs-${{ hashFiles('.lfs-
      assets-id') }}
  - name: Git LFS Pull
    run: |
      git lfs pull
      git add .
      git reset --hard
  - name: Cache Library
    uses: actions/cache@v2
    with:
      path: Library
      key: Library-Test
      restore-keys: |
        Library-
  - name: Run test ${{ matrix.testMode }}
    uses: game-ci/unity-test-runner@v2
    id: tests
    env:
```

```
        UNITY_LICENSE: ${{ secrets.UNITY_LICENSE }}
      with:
        testMode: ${{ matrix.testMode }}
        artifactsPath: ${{ matrix.testMode }}-artifacts
        githubToken: ${{ secrets.GITHUB_TOKEN }}
        checkName: ${{ matrix.testMode }} Test Results
    - name: Upload artifact for test in ${{ matrix.testMode }}
      uses: actions/upload-artifact@v2
      if: always()
      with:
        name: Test results for ${{ matrix.testMode }}
        path: ${{ steps.tests.outputs.artifactsPath }}
build:
  name: Build - ${{ matrix.targetPlatform }}
  runs-on: ubuntu-latest
  strategy:
    fail-fast: false
    matrix:
      targetPlatform:
        - StandaloneOSX
        - WebGL

  steps:
    - name: Checkout code
      uses: actions/checkout@v2
    - name: Create LFS file list
      run: git lfs ls-files -l | cut -d' ' -f1 | sort > .lfs-
      assets-id
    - name: Restore LFS cache
      uses: actions/cache@v2
      id: lfs-cache
      with:
```

```
    path: .git/lfs
    key: ${{ runner.os }}-lfs-${{ hashFiles
    ('.lfs-assets-id') }}
- name: Git LFS Pull
  run: |
    git lfs pull
    git add .
    git reset --hard
- name: Cache Library
  uses: actions/cache@v2
  with:
    path: Library
    key: Library-${{ matrix.targetPlatform }}
    restore-keys: Library-
- name: Build for ${{ matrix.targetPlatform }}
  uses: game-ci/unity-builder@v2
  env:
    UNITY_LICENSE: ${{ secrets.UNITY_LICENSE }}
  with:
    targetPlatform: ${{ matrix.targetPlatform }}
```

Deploying Artifacts

Deploying artifacts with a CI is not a big mystery, and it is less of a mystery when you can combine Unity, Wasm, WebGL, GitHub Actions, and GitHub Pages. In this example you will deploy an artifact to GitHub Pages, but the mechanics of doing so is similar in any platform:

1. Generate a build to the target platform in your CI.

2. Store that build somewhere.

3. Have the platform deployment credentials stored in your CI.

4. Run a script that can deploy the build with the correct credentials in the target platform.

For the GitHub Actions to deploy to GitHub Pages, you need to build a Unity targeting WebGL, which you already did in the Build ➤ Strategy ➤ Matrix ➤ targetPlatform ➤ WebGL script. However, you still need to store the built artifact somewhere, which you can do by adding the code in Listing 15-15 to the build script.

Listing 15-15. GitHub Actions Upload Build Artifact

```
- name: Build for ${{ matrix.targetPlatform }}
  ...
- uses: actions/upload-artifact@v2
  with:
    name: build-${{ matrix.targetPlatform }}
    path: build/${{ matrix.targetPlatform }}
```

Basically this means that after you build the artifact for matrix. targetPlatform, you will use the actions/upload-artifact@v2 action to upload the artifact called build-${{ matrix.targetPlatform }} in the path build/${{ matrix.targetPlatform }}. Now you need to configure GitHub Pages to make your WebGL build available.

Configuring GitHub Pages

The first thing you need to do to use GitHub Pages is create a GitHub Pages branch, which I usually call gh-pages. You can then enable GitHub Pages in your repository by going to Settings ➤ Pages. For the purposes here, the only important fields are Sources and the Enforce HTTPS checkbox.

Enforce HTTPS forces your page to us HTTPS, while Sources is where the configuration actually happens. You can see that your sources have a Branch dropdown. Choose the branch where your built items will be available; in this case, it's gh-pages. Then choose the folder where your build will be. You usually have only two options—/root and /docs—I usually deploy to root. Click the Save button. The Custom Domain option is when you have a hosted domain that you want the code to be deployed to and Theme is the theme style that you want your GitHub Pages to have. For GitHub Pages WebGL projects on Unity, make sure to set the Publishing Compression Format to Disabled. To do this, choose File ➤ Build Settings ➤ Player Settings. Then click the WebGL icon and choose Publishing Settings ➤ Compression Format.

The Deploy Script

The deploy script cannot be executed before (or in parallel with) the build script, as it requires an uploaded build to generate its deployment. To make sure of this order, you tag the deploy script with needs: build, then you give it a name and set it to run in Linux, as shown in Listing 15-16.

Listing 15-16. GitHub Actions Deploy Build Base Script

```
```
deployPages:
   needs: build
   name: Deploy to GitHub Pages 🚀
   runs-on: ubuntu-latest
   steps: …
```
```

You must download the artifact from the storage and run an action to deploy it in GitHub Pages. You can do that with the actions in Listing 15-17.

Listing 15-17. GitHub Actions Complete Deploy Build Script

```
```
deployPages:
    ...
    steps:
        - name: Checkout code
          uses: actions/checkout@v2
        - uses: actions/download-artifact@v2
          with:
            name: build-WebGL
            path: build
        - name: Deploy 🚀
          uses: JamesIves/github-pages-deploy-action@4.1.4
          with:
            branch: gh-pages
            folder: build/WebGL
```
```

Now, check the GitHub Pages and play. The link to your GitHub Pages can be found in your repository by going to Settings ➤ Pages.

One important note is that, to deploy to Android and iOS, some packaging conventions may be required. For Android, the package must be named com.YourCompanyName.YourProductName. More information about deploying to platforms can be found at Game CI. The next chapter explores how to develop a character controller script in Unity using TDD.

Summary

This chapter showed you how to configure Unity to support Edit Mode and Play Mode tests, as well as how to configure GitHub Actions to work as your project CI for Unity. The configuration tests the code, builds multiple platforms, and deploys the build in GitHub Pages.

CHAPTER 16

Testing Gameplay

How do you develop a character controller with TDD?

There are many character controller implementations you can use to simplify your project's development, and there is no shame in using them, especially the well tested ones. Just be sure to test your code. This chapter explores how to develop a character controller using Unity's standard `CharacterController` component and test-driven development for the gameplay behaviors usually associated with a character. It starts by detecting mouse and keyboard inputs, then a first person camera, movement, and gravity. This will be all deployed in the GitHub Pages[1] for demo purposes and the source code[2] is available on my GitHub.

Testing Keyboard Input

Keyboards, mice, and gamepads are the core of most gaming experiences. In online games, they usually provide the information that is sent to the server, while in local games, they manage how the characters move and which actions they take. Therefore, it makes a lot of sense to start your testing scenarios with keyboard input.

---

[1] https://naomijub.github.io/FPSwithTDD/
[2] https://github.com/naomijub/FPSwithTDD

© Julia Naomi Rosenfield Boeira 2024
J. N. Rosenfield Boeira, *Lean Game Development*,
https://doi.org/10.1007/978-1-4842-9843-5_16

Create a Moving Script with Rigidbody

I usually like to start explaining how to use TDD for games in reverse order: "Create the expected script and then start thinking about the changes that testing would cause." I do this because many game developers are not experienced with testing, so it helps to set the value of testing and improves the ability to write tests.

Having said that, the following is the usual flow for a moving script with a Rigidbody. You can assume that the object moves based on the input key; in this case, it's the WASD keys.

1. Create a scene with a plane and a cube, put the cube above the plane, and add colliders to both of them. It helps to have different colors for each. See Figure 16-1.

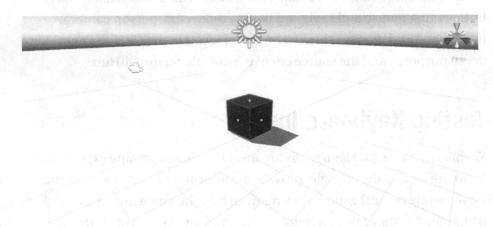

Figure 16-1. *Scene with a black cube and a white plane colliding*

2. To the cube, add a Rigidbody. Choose Add Component ➤ Physics ➤ Rigidbody.

3. Go to the Scripts folder and create a new script, which I called CubeMovementController. You can find it by choosing Create ➤ C# Script ➤ CubeMovementController. Drag and drop the CubeMovementController script to the cube or choose Add Component ➤ Scripts ➤ CubeMovementController. See Listing 16-1.

Listing 16-1. The CubeMovementController Script

```
```
using System.Collections;
using System.Collections.Generic;
using UnityEngine;

public class CubeMovementController : MonoBehaviour
{
    [SerializeField]
    private float speed = 20f;
    Rigidbody _rb;

    void Start() {
        _rb = GetComponent<Rigidbody>();
    }

    void Update() {
        var h = Input.GetAxis("Horizontal");
        var v = Input.GetAxis("Vertical");
        float x = h * speed * Time.deltaTime;
        float z = v * speed * Time.deltaTime;
```
```

```
    _rb.MovePosition(transform.position + new
    Vector3(x, 0, z));
  }
}
```

Great! Now the cube moves perfectly in the x and z directions. However, the problem with this script is the use of static and impure methods like Input.GetAxis and Time.deltaTIme, because you can't define their output values as needed for testing. To start testing, you need a function that allows you to isolate this issue of not controlling the output values. h and v are already somehow isolated in variables so that you can pass them as functions, but you still need to deal with Time.deltaTime. The pattern that you will use to deal with this is named *Humble Object Pattern*.

Testing with the Humble Object Pattern

Humble object pattern is a common design pattern applied to game development when a component has non-trivial logic, like static impure functions. It is especially used for framework-derived function testing and extending. In this case, the respective framework would be the game engine Unity.

The objective of this pattern is to strip all the logic that is not testable or is poorly testable from the function to be tested and organize it in a way so that it becomes easier to test. Having said that, the first step is to extract the Time.deltaTime call to an argument being passed to a new function, called speedByFrame. You will be responsible for defining the object's speed movement in the current frame. Change DemoTestScript. cs to CubeMovementControllerTest.cs and write a test that returns the expected frame speed for a given deltaTime, as shown in Listing 16-2.

Listing 16-2. Testing speedByFrame when deltaTime Is Positive

```
using NUnit.Framework;
using UnityEngine;

public class CubeMovementControllerTest
{
    GameObject go;

    [SetUp]
    public void SetUp()
    {
        go = new GameObject("test");
        go.AddComponent<CubeMovementController>();
    }

    [Test]
    public void SpeedByFrame_WhenDeltaTimeIsPositive_
    ReturnsSpeed() {
        // Arrange
        float deltaTime = 1f;
CubeMovementController moveController = go.GetComponent<CubeMov
ementController>();

        // Act
        float actualSpeed = moveController.
        SpeedByFrame(deltaTime);

        // Assert
        Assert.AreEqual(actualSpeed, 20f);
    }

}
```

Now you have a compile problem, so to execute this test, you need to define SpeedByFrame. See Listing 16-3.

Listing 16-3. Empty Definition for SpeedByFrame

```
public float SpeedByFrame(float deltaTime) {
    return 0f;
}
```

This test happily fails, so you can assume that there is something to improve in the code. The needed improvement is to change the return value to the expected value, return speed;. With this change, you can see that the test passes, but it is not very significant. You can create a new test based on the first one that has a deltaTime of 0.3f and an expected speed of 6f. See Listing 16-4.

Listing 16-4. New Test with More Realistic Values

```
[Test]
public void SpeedByFrame_WhenDeltaTimeIsPositive_
ReturnsSpeedInTheFrame() {
    float deltaTime = 0.3f;
    CubeMovementController moveController = go.GetComponent<Cube
    MovementController>();

    float actualSpeed = moveController.SpeedByFrame(deltaTime);

    Assert.AreEqual(actualSpeed, 6f);
}
```

This test adds a new test scenario, which causes the test pipeline to fail. A new failing test is a good sign, because it means that you need to review your code. To make the test pass, you need the SpeedByFrame function to multiply speed by deltaTime. See Listing 16-5.

Listing 16-5. SpeedByFrame Considering deltaTime

```
public float SpeedByFrame(float deltaTime) {
    return speed * deltaTime;
}
```

The next step is to have SpeedByFrame consider the movement axis values. As a general rule, you can assume the values of -1f, 0f, and 1f for the axis value. SpeedByFrame needs an axis argument, so change the existing test and function to consider this value; see Listing 16-6.

Listing 16-6. Adding an Axis Value to the Tests and Function

```
[Test]
public void SpeedByFrame_WhenDeltaTimeAndAxisArePositive_
ReturnsSpeedInFrame() {
    float deltaTime = 0.3f;
    float axis = 1f;
    CubeMovementController moveController = go.GetComponent<Cube
    MovementController>();

    float actualSpeed = moveController.SpeedByFrame(deltaTime);

    Assert.AreEqual(actualSpeed, 6f);
}
```

```
public float SpeedByFrame(float axis, float deltaTime) {
    return speed * deltaTime;
}
```

The next step is to check if the speed in the frame is correct when the axis value is 0f. See Listing 16-7.

Listing 16-7. The Axis Value Is 0f

```
[Test]
public void SpeedByFrame_WhenAxisIsZero_Returns0f()
{
    float deltaTime = 0.3f;
    float axis = 0f;
    CubeMovementController moveController = go.GetComponent<Cube
    MovementController>();

    float actualSpeed = moveController.SpeedByFrame(axis,
    deltaTime);

    Assert.AreEqual(actualSpeed, 0f);
}
```

Again, the test fails, so there is some relevant work to do. To make this test pass, you need to multiply the current speed in the frame by axis, as shown in Listing 16-8.

Listing 16-8. Using the axis Value

```
```
public float SpeedByFrame(float axis, float deltaTime) {
    return speed * axis * deltaTime;
}
```
```

With these changes, you can modify the Update function to include the new SpeedByFrame method, as shown in Listing 16-9.

Listing 16-9. Update the Function Using SpeedByFrame

```
```
void Update()   {
    var h = Input.GetAxis("Horizontal");
    var v = Input.GetAxis("Vertical");
    float x = SpeedByFrame(h, Time.deltaTime);
    float z = SpeedByFrame(v, Time.deltaTime);
    _rb.MovePosition(transform.position + new Vector3(x, 0, z));
}
```
```

One important note is that comparing floats may result in floating point approximation problems. To solve that, you can use something like the Mathf.Approximately(float, float) function, which can be asserted with Assert.That(Mathf.Approximately(float1, float2)). Another possible refactor is to simplify SpeedByFrame to use expression body syntax: public float SpeedByFrame(float axis, float deltaTime) => speed * axis * deltaTime;.

Humbly Moving the Cube

There are two ways to move the cube. The first one is to generate a new Vector3 variable and add it to the current player position. The second way is to use dependency injection to control Time.deltaTime and Input. GetAxis and create an integration UnityTest. For testing purposes, we will use the first approach first and then upgrade to the dependency injection approach, so you can use which one you prefer later.

First create a new method to calculate the cube's new position, called CalculatePosition. This method will receive as an argument the current position (the x and z of the direction to move) and then will return a Vector3 of the new position. For the first test, you can make sure the position is unchanged if x and z are zero. See Listing 16-10.

Listing 16-10. Testing for Change in the Cube Position

```
[Test]
public void CalculatePostion_WhenXZAreZero_ReturnSamePosition()
{
    Vector3 originalPosition = Vector3.zero;
    CubeMovementController moveController = go.GetComponent<Cube
    MovementController>();

    Vector3 movedPosition = moveController.CalculatePosition(ori
    ginalPosition, 0f, 0f);

    Assert.AreEqual(originalPosition, movedPosition);
}
```

To make this test pass, after compiling, you can just return the position passed as the first argument public Vector3 CalculatePosition(Vector3 position, float x, float z) =>

position;. Great, the next test should be to calculate the new position when x is positive. See Listing 16-11.

Listing 16-11. Testing When x Is Positive

```
[Test]
public void CalculatePostion_WhenXIsPositive_
ReturnIncreasedXAxisPosition(){
    Vector3 originalPosition = Vector3.zero;
    float x = 1f;
    CubeMovementController moveController = go.GetComponent<Cube
    MovementController>();

    Vector3 movedPosition = moveController.CalculatePosition(ori
    ginalPosition, x, 0f);

    Assert.AreEqual(Vector3.right, movedPosition);
}
```

To make this test pass, you can just add a Vector3 with the x value to the original position, public Vector3 CalculatePosition(Vector3 position, float x, float z) => position + new Vector3(x, 0f, 0f);. Lastly, you can test the case in which z is positive as well. See Listing 16-12.

Listing 16-12. Testing When z Is Positive

```
[Test]
public void CalculatePostion_WhenXandZArePositive_
ReturnIncreasedPosition(){
    Vector3 originalPosition = Vector3.zero;
```

```
float x = 2f;
float z = 2f;
CubeMovementController moveController = go.GetComponent<Cube
MovementController>();

Vector3 movedPosition = moveController.CalculatePosition(ori
ginalPosition, x, z);

Assert.AreEqual(new Vector3(2f, 0f, 2f), movedPosition);
}
```

This is easily fixed by adding the z value to the Vector3 of the
CalculatePosition, public Vector3 CalculatePosition(Vector3
position, float x, float z) => position + new Vector3(x, 0f, z);
method. With this done, you can upgrade the update method to use
CalculatePosition, as shown in Listing 16-13.

Listing 16-13. Upgraded Update Function

```
void Update() {
    var h = Input.GetAxis("Horizontal");
    var v = Input.GetAxis("Vertical");
    float x = SpeedByFrame(h, Time.deltaTime);
    float z = SpeedByFrame(v, Time.deltaTime);

    _rb.MovePosition(CalculatePosition(transform.
    position, x, z));
}
```

Dependency Injection

Currently we are only unit testing these cube movement methods, but you still need to test the interactions between the cube and the plane. For example, you need to test whether the cube really moves when an axis input is pressed. To be able to manipulate Input.GetAxis and Time. deltaTime, you need some way to control them during integration tests and you can use *interfaces* to create a substitutable object for testing. Input.GetAxis and Time.deltaTime are *unity services functions,* so you can name the interface IUnityService. Usually in C#, interfaces start with a capital letter I, such as IUnityService. This interface will have two associated methods—GetInputAxis and GetDeltaTime. See Listing 16-14.

Listing 16-14. IUnityService Interface Declaration

```
`` `

using System;
public interface IUnityService
{
    float GetDeltaTime();
    float GetInputAxis(string axis);
}
`` `
```

Now you need "something" to implement IUnityService. You could just implement it in the MonoBehaviour CubeMovementController, but this would make it a little more complicated to test, so you can add it as a new component class to CubeMovementController. To do this, you have to create a new class, named UnityService, that implements IUnityService and MonoBehaviour for the Input and Time classes and the interface that you created. See Listing 16-15.

Listing 16-15. IUnityService Implementation

```
```
using UnityEngine;

public class UnityService : MonoBehaviour, IUnityService
{
    float IUnityService.GetDeltaTime()
    {
        return Time.deltaTime;
    }
    float IUnityService.GetInputAxis(string axis)
    {
        return Input.GetAxis(axis);
    }
}
```
```

Then, in CubeMovementController, you need to add a new attribute called public IUnityService unityService. See Listing 16-16.

Listing 16-16. Applying IUnityService to CubeMovementController

```
```
using UnityEngine;

public class CubeMovementController : MonoBehaviour
{
    public IUnityService unityService;

    [SerializeField]
    private float speed = 20f;
    Rigidbody _rb;
```
```

```
void Start()  {
    _rb = GetComponent<Rigidbody>();
}

void Update()  {
    var h = unityService.GetInputAxis("Horizontal");
    var v = unityService.GetInputAxis("Vertical");
    var deltaTime = unityService.GetDeltaTime();
    float x = SpeedByFrame(h, deltaTime);
    float z = SpeedByFrame(v, deltaTime);

    _rb.MovePosition(CalculatePosition(transform.
    position, x, z));
}

public float SpeedByFrame(float axis, float deltaTime) =>
speed * axis * deltaTime;

public Vector3 CalculatePosition(Vector3 position, float x,
float z) => position + new Vector3(x, 0f, z);
}
```

There are a few options for instantiating this unityService attribute:

- Add the UnityService script to the component and, in the Start function, get its content with unityService = GetComponent<IUnityService>().

- For testing purposes, you could create a constructor to CubeMovementController and pass a mock implementation of IUnityService as an argument.

- Check if unityService is not null, and if it is null,
  construct a new UnityService and add to it. I know it
  is not a great practice in C# to use if something ==
  null or call constructors in Unity, but it can be a useful
  alternative.

This chapter implements the first choice, as I want to avoid using
constructors in Unity. You can use this to test it in Play Mode.

Play Mode Tests

Play Mode tests execute a pseudo-unity scene, so they allow you to directly
test behaviors during play time, supporting Start, Awake, and Update
methods. Because you have interfaces, you can replace the interface
method according to your needs in the test. Usually, to simplify test
arrangements, you would use a test double library like NSubstitute. There
are a few tutorials online on how to include them in Unity, but in this
book I avoid anything not included in Unity. To do that, you will need to
generate a new IUnityService mock implementation for each of your test
objectives. Thankfully it isn't a lot.

Now you need to create a playmode test folder with an assembly
definition for Play Mode tests. It is just like you did for Edit Mode, but
in the playmode section of the test runner. So, in the Assets folder, go
to the test runner and choose Create PlayMode Test Assembly Folder. I
named it PlayTests. Then click Create Test Script in the current folder. I
named it CubeMovementTest. The first test consists only of testing if any
movement happens when some input is added. To do this, you first need
to implement a IUnityService mock that will return predictable values.
So you create a C# script in PlayTests named FakeUnityService. See
Listing 16-17.

Listing 16-17. IUnityService Mock Implementation

```
using UnityEngine;
public class FakeUnityService : MonoBehaviour, IUnityService
{
    float IUnityService.GetDeltaTime() => 0.3f;

    float IUnityService.GetInputAxis(string axis)
    {
        if (axis == "Horizontal")
        {
            return 1f;
        }
        else
        {
            return -1f;
        }
    }
}
```

FakeUnityService is pretty simple and easy to use. What it does
is return 0.3f whenever GetDeltaTime is called. It returns 1f when
GetInpuxAxis is called with "Horizontal" and -1f for other cases.
Now you can make your first Unity integration test, which will be a little
redundant as it won't change or improve the script. This is because
you already implemented the Update function, and in a normal flow,
you would implement this test, see it fail, and then implement the
Update function. I named this test CubeMovement_OneFrameSkipped_
MovesCubePosition and it will be a UnityTest to check if the
CubeMovementController works in a single update cycle. This test will
check if given FakeUnityService, the cube will move its position when one

frame is skipped. To do that, you need to associate a GameObject and to a CubeMovementController, a Rigidbody, and a FakeUnityService. In the test, you need to get the game object's transform position as origin, skip a frame with yield return null, and then get the game object's transform new position as actual to assert they are not equal. See Listing 16-18.

Listing 16-18. Cube Movement First Integration Test

```
```
using System.Collections;
using NUnit.Framework;
using UnityEngine;
using UnityEngine.TestTools;

public class CubeMovementTest
{
    GameObject go;

    [SetUp]
    public void SetUp()
    {
        go = new GameObject("test");
        go.AddComponent<CubeMovementController>();
        go.AddComponent<Rigidbody>();
        go.AddComponent<FakeUnityService>();
    }

    [UnityTest]
    public IEnumerator CubeMovement_OneFrameSkipped_
    MovesCubePosition()
    {
        Vector3 origin = go.transform.position;

        yield return null;
        Vector3 actual = go.transform.position;
```
```

```
Assert.AreNotEqual(origin, actual);
    }
}
```

Remember that `UnityTests` should return an `IEnumerator`. A better approach would be to test if the actual x position increased, the actual z position decreased, and the actual y remained zero. This test allows you to generate a new auxiliary function that manipulates the cube movement, called `Movement`. See Listing 16-19.

Listing 16-19. Cube Movement Helper Method

```
public class CubeMovementController : MonoBehaviour
{
    // ...

    void Update()   {
        var h = unityService.GetInputAxis("Horizontal");
        var v = unityService.GetInputAxis("Vertical");
        var deltaTime = unityService.GetDeltaTime();
        Movement(h, v, deltaTime);
    }

    void Movement(float h, float v, float deltaTime)
    {
        float x = SpeedByFrame(h, deltaTime);
        float z = SpeedByFrame(v, deltaTime);

        _rb.MovePosition(CalculatePosition(transform.
        position, x, z));
    }
    // ...
}
```

225

Now, if you have a simpler Update method and can change the test function to explicitly say you are testing the Movement function, it might be interesting to also change yield return null to yield return new WaitForSeconds(0.3f) or yield return new WaitForFixedUpdate() because it would allow you to better control the results. See Listing 16-20.

Listing 16-20. Updating the Test Method

```
[UnityTest]
public IEnumerator Movement_OneFrameSkipped_MovesCubePosition()
{
    Vector3 origin = go.transform.position;

    yield return new WaitForSeconds(0.3f);
    Vector3 actual = go.transform.position;

    Assert.AreNotEqual(origin, actual);
}
```

Testing Character Controller and First-Person Camera

Before you start, a quick note on Unity's character controller. Understanding which character controller to use in your game is a little harder than "just pick anyone, they are all fine" and you need to understand their differences. Also, you need to understand what a character controller actually is and how they are different. There are basically three options for movement controllers in Unity:

- Built-in character controller

- Rigidbody (dynamic and kinematic)

- Your custom script

Needless to say, using a custom script is a terrible idea for starters or MVPs, and should only be used if the other solutions are not working for you. There is one good thing about using a custom script, which is it is highly flexible and it may be less complex than the power that you gain from its flexibility.

Character Controller

A character controller is a component, or a group of components, attached to a character that is responsible for handling character movement and physics interactions, mostly collision detection. Some other important concepts related to controlling characters are gravity, jumping, drag, in-air movement, stairs, slopes, tilting, sprinting, and crouching.

Unity's Built-in Character Controller

There is a built-in component available in the Unity editor to associate to a character, it is basically a capsule collider and a movement script developed by Unity's team, which is a wrapper over Unity's physics engine controller. It contains a list of properties and methods related to character movement, walking upstairs, walking through uneven grounds and slopes, and collision detection. It is usually the fastest implementation to set up character movement.

Rigidbody

Rigidbodies are components that interact with physics in real time. Although the built-in character controller has collision detection, it does not interact with other physics properties that a Rigidbody interacts with, such as gravity, mass, momentum, and drag. So, by adding a Rigidbody, you are "subscribing" the character into Unity's physics engine and defining that you want all physics forces to be applied by default.

Additionally, if you add *colliders* to the character, the physics engine will detect collisions to all other bodies that have colliders. Rigidbodies with colliders have a key property, which is `isKinematic`. When this property is unchecked, the Rigidbody is considered dynamic, like the one in the previous chapter, and when it is checked it is considered kinematic. Basically a kinematic Rigidbody disregards default physics forces and it is not moved by default collisions, so you are telling Unity that you will handle how this body collides and interacts with physics by a custom script. One thing that I suggest before continuing is to play with a Rigidbody in both modes by throwing stuff at it, rapidly colliding it with walls, and adding different forces to it.

Differences Between a Built-In Character Controller and a Rigidbody

- Rigidbodies interact with other physics objects, possibly moving them in collision, while a built-in character controller does not physically interact with them.

- Gravity is not automatically applied to a built-in controller. They only move when your code tells them to. However, the `SimpleMove` method does apply gravity.

- Rigidbodies have drag applied to them by default.

- There is no momentum or drag for the movement, so there is no outside force to accelerate or decelerate a built-in controller.

- Built-in character controllers do have a simple gravity mechanic by using the SimpleMove method.

- Stairs and slopes are easily walkable for the built-in controller with the correct configuration, while it will not slide down a slope if it is located in the middle of a slope. On the other hand, Rigidbodies will interact perfectly with sliding slopes, but will have a hard time interacting with stairs.

- Built-in controllers have a property that detects if they are colliding with the ground, while Rigidbodies don't. This helps with jumping mechanics. Including this mechanic in Rigidbodies is pretty simple and it may help to deal with double jumps.

- Built-in character controllers don't rotate the collider capsule, so tilting sideways may be a problem for them.

- Due to the skin width and overlap recovery properties, built-in controllers don't get stuck in walls like Rigidbodies do.

The conclusion is that neither of them is complete or works for every case, but they are definitely a good start for an MVP or even for a full game. For more information on Unity's built-in character controller, check out the reference[3] and the manual.[4] The following section includes

---

[3] https://docs.unity3d.com/ScriptReference/CharacterController.html
[4] https://docs.unity3d.com/Manual/class-CharacterController.html

a brief explanation of Unity's built-in character controller properties and most relevant methods, as well as how to apply them. This will allow you to understand which modifications you need to make to improve your character controller so that the movement and collision feels perfect for your requirements.

Let's create a scene to understand the character controller. Create a new built-in 3D scene. I named it `CharacterControllerScene` and added a plane for ground collision (choose Hierarchy ➤ 3D Objects ➤ Plane). I augmented the x and z scale to 10. Now add a capsule to the scene and increase its y so that it doesn't collide with the plane (choose Hierarchy ➤ 3D Objects ➤ Capsule, in the capsule transform, increase its y to `1.1`). Now click the capsule game object and create a new colorful material, to make the capsule more visible.

To add a character controller, go to the capsule game object and choose Add Component ➤ Physics ➤ Character Controller. Note that you now have a character controller and a capsule collider (if you have another capsule collider that you added previously, you can delete it). In the character controller, there are a few float serialized fields that you will soon explore:

- Slope limit
- Step offset
- Skin width
- Min move distance
- Center
- Radius
- Height

Also, don't forget to add some stairs and slopes by adding cubes all around. My simple scene objects are shown in Figure 16-2.

Figure 16-2. *Character controller test scene objects*

Character Controller Properties

Slope limit: This is a simple property that determines the angle, in degrees, that your character will be able to climb when moving. The character cannot walk through any slope with a higher value than the slope limit.

Step offset: This property refers to the height of a colliding object's collider that the character can mount and climb. It is measured from the bottom of your character's collider to the height of the object that it is colliding with. So, if the height of the object is higher than the step offset, the character will not be able to climb it, but if it is smaller, the character will be able to climb. Note that this property is usually between one fourth and two thirds of the character's height.

Skin width: This is one of the most interesting character controller properties, in my opinion. It is designed to prevent your character from penetrating and getting stuck in other colliders and it varies according to the direction of collision. So, for a head-on collision, when the movement direction is perpendicular to the object's direction, it is the first actual collider, preventing your character from moving forward. However, when the movement is parallel to the colliding object's direction, the skin width is ignored. When the character collides at an angle with an object's

231

collider, direction is a combination of both cases, so it will allow some overlap. The documentation of the character controller suggests it should be around 10 percent of the radius value.

Min move distance: This is the smallest change in distance that your character is required to make to actually cause a movement. This property usually has a very low value, commonly set to zero, but it exists to remove potential jitters from online games. Another case in which this property can be used is to manage the character's movement when the associated speed can have small variances and your character is not required to move. Imagine you add a stopping velocity force that results in a tiny negative velocity; this property would prevent the character moving more or moving backward.

Unity documentation has move properties that are accessible by script, including detect collision, is grounded, velocity, enable overlap recovery, and collision flags.

Detect collision: This property is a Boolean that enables or disables collisions from incoming Rigidbodies, like bullets, and will allow your character controller's collider to avoid impacting Rigidbodies. When disabled and the character is idle, the Rigidbody will pass through it. But if a move method, like move and simple move, is being called, your character will step over the incoming Rigidbody. When enabled, all collisions are detected normally. You can use this property whenever your character is required to perform an animation that would conflict with its collider, like riding in a car that has its own collider.

Enable overlay recovery: A property that is enabled by default, it helps the character controller de-penetrate static game objects and colliders when an overlap is detected. This property will make Unity push out the character from the penetrated collider when, and only when, a move method is called.

Collision flags: For me, this is one of the more complicated properties. It tells you where the collision occurred with your character in the last movement call, so if there is no movement, the associated collision region flag will not be true. It uses flags to communicate where the collision was detected. Its values are None, for no collision, Above for the top of the collider, Below for the bottom, and Sides for the middle/body. The last important note is that Sides doesn't inform you from which side the collision was detected, only that it was detected in the middle of the character.

IsGrounded: This property is linked to the Below collision flag, and it indicates that your character is colliding with something below them.

Velocity: This property tells you the velocity that your character has from the character controller's movement methods, which will be zero if the velocity is coming from outside sources, like moving pads or cars.

Character Controller Methods

There are two public movement methods in the character controller, Move and SimpleMove. Both of them take as an argument a Vector3, which is the direction change that the character controller must have. There are a few noticeable differences between them, for example:

- SimpleMove is frame-rate independent, which means the Vector3 you pass to it is probably multiplied by Time.deltaTime. It also applies gravity by default and disregards y-axis movement because of that. It is not a good method for things like jumping.

- Move is frame-rate dependent, so be sure to multiply it by Time.deltaTime to avoid weird behaviors. It doesn't apply gravity. It requires you to develop your own gravity logic and use Time.deltaTime to make it frame-rate independent.

Another important method associated with movement methods is OnControllerColliderHit, which is similar to MonoBehaviour's OnCollisionEnter and gives you access to the object hitting the character when the movement methods are called. It allows you to program custom reactions to some collisions. Now you can start testing your character controller movement. Let's start with the Camera movement.

Testing a First Person Camera

This is the base of most games. The camera is the view of the game, so you need to test the first person camera. The first step is to create a new camera under the character controller object or drag the main camera under the player—the capsule that you created previously. I also added the tag and the name player to the capsule. Avoid having two cameras on your game. I dragged the camera to the player and in the main camera transform. I clicked the three vertical dots and chose Reset so that the camera is positioned within the player's position and pointing to the character's z axis direction. Another interesting thing to do is to move the camera to the top of the capsule object, as it becomes more realistic to the sight of the player. My camera's y position is now 1.0. This will ensure that the camera's position is always subordinate to the player's position.

To understand how the look script will work, it is important to remember that everything will be handled with the mouse. The mouse can be moved into the x and y axes. If you move your player in the x axis, you want the entire player to rotate around the y axis, but if you move your mouse in the y axis, you only want the camera to rotate in the x axis, not the entire player. This allows you to rotate the player to look sideways and the player's eyes to look up and down. As the head is unable to rotate too much in the x axis, the camera rotation when looking up and down will be limited to around 180 degrees, which is called *clamping*. I created a test script for this, called CameraMovementTest in Play Mode. The first thing that you need to do is declare a GameObject that has the game object containing the Camera component and a new script called CameraMovementController, something like Listing 16-21.

Listing 16-21. Setup Camera Movement Test

```
GameObject go;

[SetUp]
public void SetUp()
{
    go = new GameObject("player");
    go.AddComponent<CameraMovementController>();
}
```

CameraMovementController needs to have a Camera. You can create a test for that using the code in Listing 16-22.

Listing 16-22. The CameraMovementController Script Contains a Camera

```
[UnityTest]
public IEnumerator CameraMovementController_WhenInstantiated_
ContainsCamera()
{
    yield return null;

    Camera expected = go.GetComponentInChildren<Camera>();
    Camera actual = go.GetComponent<CameraMovementController>().
    GetCamera();

    Assert.IsNotNull(expected);
    Assert.AreEqual(expected, actual);
}
```

What does this test mean? It means that the camera that
CameraMovementController is accessing is the same camera that
the GameObject named player contains and they are not null. Sadly,
this test fails to compile. To fix that, you can add a Camera property to
CameraMovementController, as shown in Listing 16-23.

Listing 16-23. CameraMovementController Property for Camera

```
public class CameraMovementController : MonoBehaviour
{
    public Camera Camera;
// ...
}
```

Now if you run the test in the test runner's Play Mode, you will see
that it passes, because both of them are null. This can be easily fixed by
adding a new assert that checks if the expected camera is not null: Assert.
IsNotNull(expected);. Now it fails and you can start implementing
this feature. The first thing I would do is add a Camera component to the
game object's SetUp method and see that now the failing assert is Assert.
AreEqual(expected, actual). See Listing 16-24.

Listing 16-24. Testing Setup with the Camera Component

```
[SetUp]
public void SetUp()
{
    go = new GameObject("player");
    go.AddComponent<Camera>();
    go.AddComponent<CameraMovementController>();
}
```

Note that the camera is added as a component for the player and not as a subcomponent. This is because the GameObject's GetComponentInChildren method returns the component in the GameObject or any of its children using the depth-first search. This means that if no children have the component but the game object has it, the GameObject's camera will be returned. The current test failing diff is shown in Listing 16-25.

Listing 16-25. Contains Camera Test Diff

```
Expected: <player (UnityEngine.Camera)>
But was:  null
```

This means that it is retrieving the Camera component added to SetUp while the Camera property is still null. So, in the Start method (this is why this test is in Play Mode), in CameraMovementController, you use the previously mentioned method GetComponentInChildren to set the Camera property to be the same. See Listing 16-26.

Listing 16-26. Testing the Camera to Ensure the Camera Movement Controller Is the GameObject's Camera

```
public class CameraMovementTest
{
    GameObject go;
    // ...

    [UnityTest]
    public IEnumerator CameraMovementController_
    WhenInstantiated_ContainsCamera()
```

```
    {
        yield return null;

        Camera expected = go.GetComponentInChildren<Camera>();
        Camera actual = go.GetComponent<CameraMovementControll
        er>().Camera;

        Assert.IsNotNull(expected);
        Assert.AreEqual(expected, actual);
    }
}
```

The implementation for this test is shown in Listing 16-27.

Listing 16-27. CameraMovementController Script Camera
Definition

```
public class CameraMovementController : MonoBehaviour
{
    public Camera Camera;

    void Start()
    {
        Camera = GetComponentInChildren<Camera>();
    }
}
```

There is something I really don't like with this test solution, which is
that the Camera property is public and accessible/settable from any script.
To fix that, you need to change its visibility to private and create a method,

GetCamera, that accesses the camera. The test changes to Camera actual = go.GetComponent<CameraMovementController>().GetCamera() and the CameraMovementController is shown in Listing 16-28.

Listing 16-28. The GetCamera Implementation

```
public class CameraMovementController : MonoBehaviour
{
    private Camera Camera;
    // ...
    public Camera GetCamera() {
        return Camera;
    }
}
```

This change gives you some protection over the Camera property. You now know that you own a camera in the script, so you can start the x axis camera movement.

X Axis Rotating Movement

For the mouse x axis camera movement, you have to consider a few things. First, you want it to be frame independent, so you need to consider Time. deltaTime. Secondly, you can have a property that determines mouse sensitivity. So you can start by having an Edit Mode test that returns the correct mouse x rotation for the specific sensitivity and delta time. The test is simply a method call to MouseXRotation passing as arguments the mouseX value and the delta time. It will return a multiplication containing the sensitivity over x. I called this MouseRotationTest, as shown in Listing 16-29.

Listing 16-29. Mouse Rotation Sensitivity Test

```
```
using NUnit.Framework;
using UnityEngine;

public class MouseRotationTest
{
    GameObject go;

    [SetUp]
    public void SetUp()
    {
        go = new GameObject("player");
        go.AddComponent<CameraMovementController>();
    }

    [Test]
    public void MouseXRotation_HasCorrectSensitivity()
    {
        float mouseX = 45f;
        float deltaTime = 0.015f;
        CameraMovementController movementController = go.GetComp
        onent<CameraMovementController>();

        float xRotation = movementController.
        MouseXRotation(mouseX, deltaTime);
        Assert.AreEqual(xRotation, 67.5f);
    }
}
```
```

For this test to compile, you have to create a method named
MouseXRotation that returns a float (for now, 0f is enough). The first step
to fixing this test is to make MouseXRotation return mouseX * deltaTime.

It still fails, so you create a public property named sensitivity. It will be the sensitivity in the x axis. Multiply it by mouseX * deltaTime. This property has a default value of 100f. See Listing 16-30.

Listing 16-30. Mouse Rotation Sensitivity

```
public class CameraMovementController : MonoBehaviour
{
    public float sensitivityX = 100f;
    private Camera Camera;
    // ...
    public float MouseXRotation(float mouseX, float deltaTime){
        return mouseX * sensitivityX * deltaTime;
    }
}
```

Nice, but the camera is far from moving, so now you need a Play Mode test that ensures that the player has a rotation compatible with MouseXRotation. To do this, create a test that sets the transform rotation to Quaternion.zero and then waits one second to determine if the rotation has changed. In this case, it compares it to a negative value, due to how you configured the IUnityService fake. See Listing 16-31.

Listing 16-31. Testing if the Camera Has Rotated

```
[UnityTest]
public IEnumerator RotateXCamera_WhenSecondsPass_
HasRotatedPlayerOnYAxis()
{
```

```
go.transform.rotation = Quaternion.Euler(Vector3.zero);
var originalYRotation = go.transform.rotation.y;
yield return new WaitForSeconds(1f);

var newYRotation = go.transform.rotation.y;
float actual = newYRotation - originalYRotation;

Assert.Less(actual, 0f);
}
```

There are a few changes that you need to think about to make this test pass. The first one is the dependency on Time.deltaTime, and the second one is that you need to access the mouse axis position, which can be done using the same strategy used for IUnityService. For this purpose, you can change GetInputAxis from FakeUnityService, so the method will return 45f for the mouse x and -45f for the y axis. See Listing 16-32.

Listing 16-32. FakeUnityService Method GetInputAxis Update

```
public float GetInputAxis(string axis)
{
    if (axis == "Horizontal") {
        return 1f;
    } else if (axis == "Vertical") {
        return -1f;
    } else if (axis == "Mouse X") {
        return 45f;
    } else { return 0f; }
}
```

45f is a symbolic value to simplify the test; I am not giving it any meaning for now. Also, don't forget to add IUnityServive unityService to CameraControllerMovement, assign it in the Start method with GetComponent, and add it to the player inspector. Now you can implement a rotation method, which I called RotationX. See Listing 16-33.

Listing 16-33. Camera Rotation Code Implementation

```
```
public class CameraMovementController : MonoBehaviour
{
    public float sensitivityX = 100f;
    private Camera Camera;
    private IUnityService unityService;

    void Start()
    {
        Camera = GetComponentInChildren<Camera>();
        unityService = GetComponent<IUnityService>();
    }

    void Update()
    {
        float mouseX = unityService.GetInputAxis("Mouse X");
        float deltaTime = unityService.GetDeltaTime();
        RotateX(mouseX, deltaTime);
    }

    void RotateX(float mouseX, float deltaTime)
    {
```
```

```
    float mouseRotation = MouseXRotation(mouseX, deltaTime);
    transform.Rotate(Vector3.up * mouseRotation);
  }
  // ...
}
```

Y Axis Rotating Movement

You could do the exact same thing to rotate the camera along the y axis.
However, you would then not have control over the 180 degrees rotation
limit, so you need a way to extend the rotation logic. Instead, copy the
MouseXRotation_HasCorrectSensitivity test and apply it to y with a
different sensitivity. I personally think that y sensitivity can differ from
x sensitivity. Create MouseYRotation_HasCorrectSensitivity in an Edit
Mode test called MouseRotationTest. See Listing 16-34.

Listing 16-34. Rotation Sensitivity Along the Y Axis

```
[Test]
public void MouseYRotation_HasCorrectSensitivity()
{
    float mouseY = 45f;
    float deltaTime = 0.015f;
    CameraMovementController movementController = go.GetComponent
    <CameraMovementController>();

    float yRotation = movementController.MouseYRotation(mouseY,
    deltaTime);

    Assert.AreEqual(yRotation, 54f);
}
```

As expected, the test doesn't compile, so copy MouseXRotation by changing x to y. Now the test fails. To make it pass, add a new variable called sensitivityY with the value of 80f. See Listing 16-35.

Listing 16-35. Implementing Rotation Along the Y Axis

```
public class CameraMovementController : MonoBehaviour
{
    public float sensitivityX = 100f;
    public float sensitivityY = 80f;
    // ...

    public float MouseXRotation(float mouseX, float deltaTime) {
        return mouseX * sensitivityX * deltaTime;
    }

    public float MouseYRotation(float mouseY, float deltaTime)
    {
        return mouseY * sensitivityY * deltaTime;
    }
}
```

Although these methods look odd, they are basically the same thing, but for x and y. To deal with this, you can pass sensitivity as an argument and merge the methods by changing the name to MouseRotation. See Listing 16-36.

Listing 16-36. Refactoring Mouse Rotation

```
public class CameraMovementController : MonoBehaviour
{
    public float sensitivityX = 100f;
    public float sensitivityY = 80f;
    // ...
    void RotateX(float mouseX, float deltaTime)
    {
        float mouseRotation = MouseRotation(mouseX,
        sensitivityX, deltaTime);
        transform.Rotate(Vector3.up * mouseRotation);
    }

    public float MouseRotation(float mouseAxis, float
    axisSensitivity, float deltaTime) {
        return mouseAxis * axisSensitivity * deltaTime;
    }
}
```

You can also make their names more explicit. See Listing 16-37.

Listing 16-37. Refactor Test to Align with the Mouse Rotation Refactor

```
public class MouseRotationTest
{
    // ...

    [Test]
    public void MouseRotation_OverYAxis_HasCorrectXSensitivity()
```

```
{
    float mouseX = 45f;
    float deltaTime = 0.015f;
    CameraMovementController movementController = go.GetComp
    onent<CameraMovementController>();

    float xRotation = movementController.
    MouseRotation(mouseX, movementController.sensitivityX,
    deltaTime);

    Assert.AreEqual(xRotation, 67.5f);
}
[Test]
public void MouseRotation_OverXAxis_HasCorrectYSensitivity()
{
    float mouseY = 45f;
    float deltaTime = 0.015f;
    CameraMovementController movementController = go.GetComp
    onent<CameraMovementController>();

    float yRotation = movementController.
    MouseRotation(mouseY, movementController.sensitivityY,
    deltaTime);

    Assert.AreEqual(yRotation, 54f);
}
}
```

Now you can create a Play Mode test to check the rotation over the x axis made by moving the mouse over the y axis. However, due to how the fake works, you need to create a new Play Mode test that contains a new fake that doesn't move on the x axis but does move on the y axis. This is because rotations can get complicated, especially if the camera is rotating in the x axis but the player is rotating in the y axis. The first test is very simple, and just checks, in a different way, if the localRotation camera has changed positively due to an update. See Listing 16-38.

Listing 16-38. Play Mode Test for Camera Rotation

```
public class CameraYMovementTest
{
    GameObject go;

    [SetUp]
    public void SetUp()
    {
        go = new GameObject("player");
        go.AddComponent<Camera>();
        go.AddComponent<CameraMovementController>();

        go.AddComponent<FakeYUnityService>();
    }

    [UnityTest]
    public IEnumerator RotateYCamera_WhenSecondsPass_
    HasRotatedPlayerOnXAxis()
    {
        var originalCameraXRotation = go.GetComponent<Camera>().
        transform.localRotation.x;
        yield return new WaitForSeconds(1f);

        var newCameraXRotation = go.GetComponent<Camera>().
        transform.localRotation.x;
```

```
    Assert.Greater(newCameraXRotation,
      originalCameraXRotation);
  }
}
```
```

FakeYUnityService now considers only the Mouse Y value, as shown
in Listing 16-39.

***Listing 16-39.*** FakeYUnityService Implementation

```

public class FakeYUnityService : MonoBehaviour, IUnityService
{
    public float GetDeltaTime() => 0.3f;

    public float GetInputAxis(string axis)
    {
        if (axis == "Horizontal") {
            return 1f;
        } else if (axis == "Vertical") {
            return -1f;
        } else if (axis == "Mouse Y") {
            return -1f;
        } else {
            return 0f;
        }
    }
}
```
```

To solve this test, you can implement the exact same solution as the rotation caused by the mouse x movement, for now. In the solution in Listing 16-40, note that the x axis direction is Vector.left. This is because the y axis is inverted in game programming. I will explain this soon.

Listing 16-40. Solving the Camera Rotation Test for RotateYCamera_WhenSecondsPass_HasRotatedPlayerOnXAxis

```
public class CameraMovementController : MonoBehaviour
{
    public float sensitivityX = 100f;
    public float sensitivityY = 80f;
    // ...

    void Update()
    {
        float mouseX = unityService.GetInputAxis("Mouse X");
        float mouseY = unityService.GetInputAxis("Mouse Y");
        float deltaTime = unityService.GetDeltaTime();
        RotateX(mouseX, deltaTime);
        RotateY(mouseY, deltaTime);
    }

    void RotateX(float mouseX, float deltaTime)
    {
        float mouseRotation = MouseRotation(mouseX,
        sensitivityX, deltaTime);
        Camera.transform.Rotate(Vector3.up * mouseRotation);
    }

    void RotateY(float mouseY, float deltaTime)
    {
```

```
      float mouseRotation = MouseRotation(mouseY,
      sensitivityY, deltaTime);
      transform.Rotate(Vector3.left * mouseRotation);
   }
}
```

However, if you test this solution, it doesn't quite work. This happens for two reasons:

- Complex rotations should be done with quaternions because they are responsible for rotation mathematics. Unity is no different.

- You are not clamping the rotation value between -90 degrees and 90 degrees. So you have to create a new test that will lock the rotation over the x axis between -90 and 90 degrees. This test sets the camera's localRotation to 89 degrees and applies a rotation to it with a one-second update, which reaches the 90 degrees limit. By applying a new update cycle, you can see that no change in rotation happens. If you get localRotation.eulerAngles in this test, you will see that the x angle is 90 degrees for both camera rotation tests. If you prefer to see clear angles, change it to eulerAngles. See Listing 16-41.

Listing 16-41. Clamping Rotation on Axis

```
[UnityTest]
public IEnumerator RotateYCamera_WhenSecondsPass_IsClamped()
{
```

```
go.GetComponent<Camera>().transform.localRotation =
Quaternion.Euler(89f, 0, 0);
yield return new WaitForSeconds(1f);

var newCameraXRotation = go.GetComponent<Camera>().
transform.localRotation.x;
Assert.Greater(newCameraXRotation, 0.69f);

yield return new WaitForSeconds(1f);

var secondNewCameraXRotation = go.GetComponent<Camera>().
transform.localRotation.x;
Assert.AreEqual(secondNewCameraXRotation,
newCameraXRotation);
}
```

The solution to this test is a little bit more complex, as it involves saving the current xRotation and clamping it. See Listing 16-42.

Listing 16-42. Rotation Clamping Implementation

```
public class CameraMovementController : MonoBehaviour
{
    public float sensitivityX = 100f;
    public float sensitivityY = 80f;
    private float xAxisRotation;
    // ...
    void Start()
    {
        Camera = GetComponentInChildren<Camera>();
        unityService = GetComponent<IUnityService>();
        xAxisRotation = 0f;
    }
```

```
void Update()
{
    float mouseX = unityService.GetInputAxis("Mouse X");
    float mouseY = unityService.GetInputAxis("Mouse Y");
    float deltaTime = unityService.GetDeltaTime();
    RotateY(mouseY, deltaTime);
    RotateX(mouseX, deltaTime);
}

void RotateY(float mouseY, float deltaTime)
{
    float mouseRotation = MouseRotation(mouseY,
    sensitivityY, deltaTime);
    xAxisRotation -= mouseRotation;
    xAxisRotation = Mathf.Clamp(xAxisRotation, -90f, 90f);

    Camera.transform.localRotation = Quaternion.
    Euler(xAxisRotation, 0f, 0f);
}
}
```

The xAxisRotation variable starts at 0f, so no rotation is associated with it, then it gets the mouse rotation from MouseRotation and decreases it from the current xAxisRotation. This decrease is needed because the y axis is inverted in the game screen, as point (0, 0) is the top-left corner of your screen and the bottom-left corner has an increased y value. Then you clamp the value of xAxisRotation to be between -90 and 90. You may change it to 70 if you prefer, so that you can transform it in a quaternion that rotates in the x axis to the camera's localRotation.

The last thing to do is add Cursor.lockState = CursorLockMode. Locked; to CameraMovementController's Start method so that the cursor is locked in the middle of the screen when starting. See Listing 16-43.

Listing 16-43. Locking the Cursor to the Center of the Screen Upon
Starting

```
public class CameraMovementController : MonoBehaviour
{
    // ...
    void Start()
    {
        Cursor.lockState = CursorLockMode.Locked;
        Cursor.visible = true;

        Camera = GetComponentInChildren<Camera>();
        unityService = GetComponent<IUnityService>();
        xAxisRotation = 0f;
    }
    // ...
}
```

Testing Character Controller Movement

The objective here is to write a movement controller script associated
with the character controller that will be as simple as possible while being
fluid. It should move the character, with gravity applied to it, climb steps
and slopes, and not get stuck on walls. Unity has two axes associated with
movement—Vertical and Horizontal—which are usually translated to
WASD keys or directional keys. The Input.GetAxis method receives as
a parameter a string, which would be "Vertical" and "Horizontal" for
the movement controller. Breaking down its values, the W and Up keys
return a vertical of 1f, the S and Down keys return a vertical of -1f, the D

and Right keys return a horizontal of `1f,` and the A and Left keys return a horizontal of `-1f`. These inputs allow you to move your character along the z axis for vertical input and along the x axis for horizontal input.

Making the Player Move

Before you start developing tests for your character movement script, it's important to plan how you will test it. See Table 16-1.

Table 16-1. Planning Test Scenarios for Player Movement

Feature	Directional Input Moves the Character	Test Type
Frame Speed Forward	When axis movement is forward, the resulting movement is frame independent and has the correct speed.	Edit Mode
Frame Speed Sideways	When axis movement is sideways, the resulting movement is frame independent and has the correct speed.	Edit Mode
Frame Movement Sideways	When axis movement is sideways, the resulting movement is frame independent and has the correct movement vector.	Edit Mode
Frame Movement Forward	When axis movement is forward, the resulting movement is frame independent and has the correct movement vector.	Edit Mode
Character Moves Forward and sideways	When an update happens with positive axis movement, the character is moved to a new position.	Play Mode
Movement Proportions on Rotating	When the player is moving and rotating, the increase over x and z positions are proportionally different.	Play Mode
Gravity	Player has gravity applied to it.	Play Mode

Let's go to the character movement script to implement these test cases. The first step is to create a test script, named MovementSpeedTest, that will handle the movement speed on the x and y axes, pressed input value, and delta time. This script will contain a game object named "player" in the variable go, and you need to add the PlayerMovementController script to that game object. See Listing 16-44.

Listing 16-44. MovementSpeedTest Setup

```
public class MovementSpeedTest
{
    GameObject go;

    [SetUp]
    public void SetUp()
    {
        go = new GameObject("Player");
        go.AddComponent<PlayerMovementController>();
    }
}
```

As it already complains that this is failing, create a script named PlayerMovementController in the scripts folder. Then you need to create a test that will simply return the x speed when you pass all arguments as 1f. See Listing 16-45.

Listing 16-45. Simple Movement on X Direction Test

```
[Test]
public void XMovementInFrame_WhenEverythingElseIs1_
ReturnsTheXSpeed()
```

```
{
    float deltaTime = 1f;
    float horizontal = 1f;

    float frameSpeed = go.GetComponent<PlayerMovementController>
    ().MovementOnX(horizontal, deltaTime);

    Assert.AreEqual(20f, frameSpeed);
}
```
```

To make this test compile, create a method on
PlayerMovementController named MovementOnX that receives an
axis value and a delta time value and then returns 0f. This test will
fail, so you can create a float-serialized field called xMovementSpeed
and make the newly created method return it. The test then passes.
Now create a test called XMovementInFrame_WhenDeltaTimeIsShort_
ReturnsTheXSpeedInTheFrame with a deltaTime of 0.1. See Listing 16-46.

*Listing 16-46.* Testing Velocity Proportional to deltaTime

```
```
[Test]
public void XMovementInFrame_WhenDeltaTimeIsShort_
ReturnsTheXSpeedInTheFrame() {
    float deltaTime = 0.1f;
    float horizontal = 1f;

 float frameSpeed = go.GetComponent<PlayerMovementController>
 ().MovementOnX(horizontal, deltaTime);

    Assert.AreEqual(2f, frameSpeed);
}
```
```
```

For this test to pass, you need to multiply the xMovementSpeed by deltaTime. This results in Listing 16-47.

Listing 16-47. Implementation of Velocity Proportional to deltaTime

```
```
public float MovementOnX(float axis, float deltaTime)
{
    return xMovementSpeed * deltaTime;
}
```
```

The last step is to create a test that has a negative direction axis. I call this XMovementInFrame_WhenHorizontalAxisIsNegative_ReturnsTheXSpeedInTheFrame. See Listing 16-48.

Listing 16-48. Testing Movement Along the Axis

```
```
[Test]
public void XMovementInFrame_WhenHorizontalAxisIsNegative_
ReturnsTheXSpeedInTheFrame() {
    float deltaTime = 0.1f;
    float horizontal = -1f;

    float frameSpeed = go.GetComponent<PlayerMovementController>
    ().MovementOnX(horizontal, deltaTime);

    Assert.AreEqual(-2f, frameSpeed);
}
```
```

To make this test pass, you need MovementOnX to return the multiplication of axis, deltaTime, and xMovementSpeed, which would make this method exactly like the CameraMovementController method called MouseRotation. Methods doing the same exact thing in different classes indicate *code smell,* meaning that there is something wrong with the code design. To solve this code smell, you can refactor the code by creating a new class called AuxFunctions and have a static method that will multiply three elements. See Listing 16-49.

Listing 16-49. Auxiliary Function for Sensitivity in Frame

```
public class AuxFunctions
{
    public static float SensitivityInFrame(float axis, float
    sensitivity, float deltaTime)
    {
        return axis * sensitivity * deltaTime;
    }
}
```

Now you can replace the test with this new function, include the two functions that were in MouseRotationTest (now deleted), and replace the MouseRotation method from CameraMovementController with AuxFunction.SensitivityInFrame in all of its occurrences. See Listing 16-50.

Listing 16-50. Improving MovementSpeedTest with AuxFunction. SensitivityInFrame

```
using System.Collections;
using System.Collections.Generic;
using NUnit.Framework;
using UnityEngine;
using UnityEngine.TestTools;
```

```
public class MovementSpeedTest
{
    GameObject go;
    PlayerMovementController moveController;
    CameraMovementController cameraController;

    [SetUp]
    public void SetUp()
    {
        go = new GameObject("Player");
        go.AddComponent<PlayerMovementController>();
        go.AddComponent<CameraMovementController>();
        moveController = go.GetComponent<PlayerMovementCont
        roller>();
        cameraController = go.GetComponent<CameraMovementCont
        roller>();
    }

    // A Test behaves as an ordinary method
    [Test]
    public void XMovementInFrame_WhenEverythingElseIs1_
    ReturnsTheXSpeed()
    {
        float deltaTime = 1f;
        float horizontal = 1f;

        float frameSpeed = AuxFunctions.
        SensitivityInFrame(horizontal, moveController.
        xMovementSpeed, deltaTime);

        Assert.AreEqual(20f, frameSpeed);
    }
```

```
[Test]
public void XMovementInFrame_WhenDeltaTimeIsShort_
ReturnsTheXSpeedInTheFrame() {
    float deltaTime = 0.1f;
    float horizontal = 1f;

    float frameSpeed = AuxFunctions.
    SensitivityInFrame(horizontal, moveController.
    xMovementSpeed, deltaTime);

    Assert.AreEqual(2f, frameSpeed);
}

[Test]
public void XMovementInFrame_WhenHorizontalAxisIsNegative_
ReturnsTheXSpeedInTheFrame() {
    float deltaTime = 0.1f;
    float horizontal = -1f;

    float frameSpeed = AuxFunctions.
    SensitivityInFrame(horizontal, moveController.
    xMovementSpeed, deltaTime);

    Assert.AreEqual(-2f, frameSpeed);
}

[Test]
public void CameraSensitivityOnX_WhenNothingIs1f_
ReturnsSensitivityOnFrame()
{
    float mouseX = 45f;
    float deltaTime = 0.015f;

    float xRotation = AuxFunctions.SensitivityInFrame(mouseX,
    cameraController.sensitivityX, deltaTime);
```

261

```
        Assert.AreEqual(xRotation, 67.5f);
    }
    [Test]
    public void CameraSensitivityOnY_WhenNothingIs1f_
    ReturnsSensitivityOnFrame()
    {
        float mouseY = 45f;
        float deltaTime = 0.015f;

        float yRotation = AuxFunctions.
        SensitivityInFrame(mouseY, cameraController.
        sensitivityY, deltaTime);

        Assert.AreEqual(yRotation, 54f);
    }
}
```

Do the same to the MonoBehaviour Camera script. Listing 16-51 shows the result.

Listing 16-51. Applying AuxFunction.SensitivityInFrame to CameraMovementController

```
public class CameraMovementController : MonoBehaviour
{
    public float sensitivityX = 100f;
    public float sensitivityY = 80f;

    // ...
    void RotateX(float mouseX, float deltaTime)
    {
```

```
    float mouseRotation = AuxFunctions.
    SensitivityInFrame(mouseX, sensitivityX, deltaTime);
    transform.Rotate(Vector3.up * mouseRotation);
}

void RotateY(float mouseY, float deltaTime)
{
    float mouseRotation = AuxFunctions.
    SensitivityInFrame(mouseY, sensitivityY, deltaTime);
    xAxisRotation -= mouseRotation;
    xAxisRotation = Mathf.Clamp(xAxisRotation, -90f, 90f);

    Camera.transform.localRotation = Quaternion.
    Euler(xAxisRotation, 0f, 0f);
}
}
```

Now that the refactoring is done, speed becomes sensitivity, as it also refers to the step that you are going to take when moving, and you have deleted some code that doesn't make sense anymore. The next step is to make MovementOnX a bit more than just a multiplier function; it can return the Vector3 associated with the change that you expect on the movement over the x axis. To do this, create a test on MovementSpeed named MovementOnX_WhenValuesAreNot1f_ReturnsNegativeRightVector3 that will receive an axis value and a delta time. It returns the x axis direction that your character should move. Note that the axis value is negative, so the expected value of MovementOnX should be a Vector3.left multiplied by the resulting multiplication from AuxFunctions.SensitivityOnFrame. See Listing 16-52.

Listing 16-52. Test to Make Movement Return a Vector3

```
[Test]
public void MovementOnX_WhenValuesAreNot1f_
ReturnsNegativeRightVector3()
{
    float axis = -1f;
    float deltaTime = 0.1f;
    Vector3 expected = Vector3.left * 2f;

    Vector3 actual = moveController.MovementOnX(axis,
    deltaTime);
    Assert.AreEqual(expected, actual);
}
```

For this test to pass, simply make MovementOnX return a Vector3.
right multiplied by the sensitivity that's calculated by AuxFunctions.
SensitivityOnFrame. See Listing 16-53.

Listing 16-53. Implementing Movement with Vector3

```
public Vector3 MovementOnX(float axis, float deltaTime)
{
    return Vector3.right * AuxFunctions.SensitivityInFrame(axis,
    xMovementSpeed, deltaTime);
}
```

Now you can use the same concept of testing for the movement on the z axis, called MovementOnZ_WhenValuesAreNot1f_ ReturnsNegativeForwardVector3. As moving forward is relatively easier than moving sideways, the assert can be equal to Vector3.back * 3.5f. See Listing 16-54.

Listing 16-54. Testing Movement When Values Are Not 1f

```
[Test]
public void MovementOnZ_WhenValuesAreNot1f_
ReturnsNegativeForwardVector3()
{
    float axis = -1f;
    float deltaTime = 0.1f;
    Vector3 expected = Vector3.back * 3.5f;

    Vector3 actual = moveController.MovementOnZ(axis,
    deltaTime);

    Assert.AreEqual(expected, actual);
}
```

Now you need to create a MovementOnZ function on PlayerMovementController that can return a simple Vector3. forward. As it doesn't pass yet, you can multiply Vector3.forward by the same value you used on MovementOnX, which is AuxFunctions. SensitivityInFrame(axis, xMovementSpeed, deltaTime). This improves the result, but it is still not quite right. To make it right, create a zMovementSpeed serialized property with the value of 35f and replace xMovementSpeed with zMovementSpeed. See Listing 16-55.

Listing 16-55. Fixing Moving Forward

```
```
public class PlayerMovementController : MonoBehaviour
{
    [SerializeField]
    public float xMovementSpeed = 20f;
    [SerializeField]
    public float zMovementSpeed = 35f;

    public Vector3 MovementOnX(float axis, float deltaTime)
    {
        return Vector3.right * AuxFunctions.
        SensitivityInFrame(axis, xMovementSpeed, deltaTime);
    }

    public Vector3 MovementOnZ(float axis, float deltaTime)
    {
        return Vector3.forward * AuxFunctions.
        SensitivityInFrame(axis, zMovementSpeed, deltaTime);
    }
}
```
```

The movement now seems to be working fine. Let's test if the character actually moves. To do that, you will create a Play Mode that checks if the new position is different from the original position and whether they have changed to the correct values. To create this test, you need a Play Mode script test named `CharacterMovementTest` and a test in it that will check if the position has changed. Note that the game object has a `FakeUnityService`, as it will require `Time.deltaTime` and `Input.GetAxis`, and `CharacterController`, which is Unity's built-in character controller script. See Listing 16-56.

Listing 16-56. Play Mode Test for Character Movement

```
using System.Collections;
using System.Collections.Generic;
using NUnit.Framework;
using UnityEngine;
using UnityEngine.TestTools;

public class CharacterMovementTest
{
    [UnityTest]
    public IEnumerator CharacterMovement_When1SecondPassed_
    MovesCharacter()
    {
        GameObject go = new GameObject("Player");
        go.AddComponent<PlayerMovementController>();
        go.AddComponent<CharacterController>();
        go.AddComponent<FakeUnityService>();
        Vector3 original = go.transform.position;

        yield return new WaitForSeconds(1f);

        Vector3 actual = go.transform.position;

        Assert.AreNotEqual(original, actual);
    }
}
```

As expected, the test fails because there is nothing being executed on
the update method. You can fix that by adding a `CharacterController`
property and a `IUnityService` property, attaching a component to them.

267

Then use `CharacterController.Move` to move the character to a new direction based on the vectorial sum of `MovementOnX` and `MovementOnZ`. See Listing 16-57.

Listing 16-57. Moving the Character as Expected

```
public class PlayerMovementController : MonoBehaviour
{
    [SerializeField]
    public float xMovementSpeed = 20f;
    [SerializeField]
    public float zMovementSpeed = 35f;

    CharacterController controller;
    IUnityService unityService;

    void Start()
    {
        controller = GetComponent<CharacterController>();
        unityService = GetComponent<IUnityService>();
    }

    void Update()
    {
        float horizontal = unityService.GetInputAxis("Horizontal");
        float vertical = unityService.GetInputAxis("Vertical");
        float deltaTime = unityService.GetDeltaTime();

        Vector3 movement = MovementOnX(horizontal, deltaTime) +
        MovementOnZ(vertical, deltaTime);

        controller.Move(movement);
    }
```

```
public Vector3 MovementOnX(float axis, float deltaTime)...

public Vector3 MovementOnZ(float axis, float deltaTime)...
}
```

You should now test this script in a real scene to see how it is working. To do that, make sure to add a `CharacterController` component and the `PlaymerMovementController` to your player. Also, don't forget what you have already added for `camera`, `UnityService`, and `CameraMovementController` and have set the camera as children to your player. Press Play and try to move a little. If you move, you will notice two problems with this code:

- Whenever you move upstairs or up a slope, the player doesn't fall. This is because the `Move` method doesn't apply gravity to this component.

- The player seems to be always moving in the same direction, no matter where they are looking.

To solve the second problem, let's create a test in `CharacterMovementTest` that executes a rotation and moves the player. I named the test `MovementAndRotation_OnRotatingView_HasZXIncreasedInDifferentProportions`. It has two `yields` in it. The first one ensures minimal movement, while the second one ensures a larger movement. The idea is to check if the proportion of movement on the x and z axes is different, because rotation would make the player deviate from a proportional path. To assist with this test, I created a new `IUnityService` called `FakeUnityServicePlayTest`. See Listings 16-58 and 16-59.

Listing 16-58. New Fake Unity Service to Consider Movement and Rotation

```
```
public class FakeUnityServicePlayTest : MonoBehaviour,
IUnityService
{
    public float GetDeltaTime() => 0.03f;

    public float GetInputAxis(string axis)
    {
        if (axis == "Horizontal")
        {
            return 0f;
        }
        else if (axis == "Vertical")
        {
            return 1f;
        }
        else if (axis == "Mouse X")
        {
            return 0.5f;
        }
        else
        {
            return 0f;
        }
    }
}
```
```

Listing 16-59. Play Mode Test to Consider Rotation and Movement

```
[UnityTest]
public IEnumerator MovementAndRotation_OnRotatingView_
HasZXIncreasedInDifferentProportions()
{
    GameObject player = new GameObject("TestPlayer");
    player.AddComponent<PlayerMovementController>();
    player.AddComponent<CharacterController>();
    player.AddComponent<FakeUnityService>();
    player.AddComponent<Camera>();
    player.AddComponent<CameraMovementController>();

    yield return new WaitForSeconds(0.1f);
    Vector3 origin = player.transform.position;

    yield return new WaitForSeconds(0.3f);

    Vector3 actual = player.transform.position;
    int xProportion = Mathf.RoundToInt(actual.x / origin.x);
    int zProportion = Mathf.RoundToInt(actual.z / origin.z);

    Assert.AreNotEqual(xProportion, zProportion);
}
```

By executing this test, you will observe that the error says that both proportions are equal to the same integer, but the zProportion should be, at least a little bit, larger than the xProportion. To solve this issue, you should fix the MonvementOn_* methods. They are using Vector3.forward and Vector3.right to determine the direction of movement, but you need this movement to be relative to the game object's transform. Change the methods as shown in Listing 16-60.

Listing 16-60. Implementation to Consider Rotation on Player Movement

```
public Vector3 MovementOnX(float axis, float deltaTime)
{
    return transform.right * AuxFunctions.
    SensitivityInFrame(axis, xMovementSpeed, deltaTime);
}

public Vector3 MovementOnZ(float axis, float deltaTime)
{
    return transform.forward * AuxFunctions.
    SensitivityInFrame(axis, zMovementSpeed, deltaTime);
}
```

Now the test is passing. However, to make this test more robust and less flaky, change the assert as shown in Listing 16-61.

Listing 16-61. Improving the Test Assertion

```
float xProportion = actual.x / origin.x;
float zProportion = actual.z / origin.z;

Assert.Greater(zProportion, xProportion);
```

The Edit Mode test continues to pass because it does not include any rotation. Now it's time address the first issue, which is that gravity is not applied.

Applying Gravity

The last step for a character controller is to apply gravity to the character. The visual effect of gravity is that the player moves down a little each frame. This is because gravity is a force applied downward over time (where the body with the largest mass, in this case the ground, is located). The other effect of gravity being applied over time is that the speed downward will increase over time, as the equation $V = Vo + g.t$ defines. (Vo is the initial velocity, g is the gravity, t is the delta time, and V is the resulting velocity.) With this in mind, your first test should be very simple. You need only to test if your player's velocity has decreased over time in the y axis. See Listing 16-62.

Listing 16-62. First Gravity Unit Test

```
public class MovementSpeedTest
{
    GameObject go;
    PlayerMovementController moveController;
    CameraMovementController cameraController;

    [SetUp]
    public void SetUp()
    {
        go = new GameObject("Player");
        go.AddComponent<PlayerMovementController>();
        go.AddComponent<CameraMovementController>();
        moveController = go.GetComponent<PlayerMovementCont
        roller>();
        cameraController = go.GetComponent<CameraMovement
        Controller>();
    }
```

```
// ...
    [Test]
    public void CalculateGravityVelocity_WhenPlayerIsNotMoving_
    DecreasesPlayerYVelocity()
    {
        Vector3 playerOriginalVelocity = moveController.
        velocity;

        moveController.CalculateGravityVelocity();

        Assert.Less(moveController.velocity.y,
        playerOriginalVelocity.y);
        Assert.AreEqual(moveController.velocity.x,
        playerOriginalVelocity.x);
        Assert.AreEqual(moveController.velocity.z,
        playerOriginalVelocity.z);
        Assert.AreEqual(moveController.velocity.z, 0f);
    }

}
```

As this is a very simple test, you can start with a very simple implementation to check if it fails and not use it in Update. Then you can improve the solution to calculate the new velocity applied to the object due to gravity. See Listing 16-63.

Listing 16-63. Calculating Gravity from the First Assert

```
public class PlayerMovementController : MonoBehaviour
{
    [SerializeField]
    public float xMovementSpeed = 20f;
```

```
[SerializeField]
public float yMovementSpeed = 35f;
[SerializeField]
public Vector3 velocity = Vector3.zero;
float gravity = -9.8f;

// ...
public void CalculateGravityVelocity()
    {
        velocity.y += gravity;
    }

}
```

The test works well, but it is not time dependent, which is something that you need to consider when applying forces. To solve that, you can add a new test that considers time dependency (remember to add deltaTime to the previous test). See Listing 16-64.

Listing 16-64. Adding a Time Dependent Test

```
[Test]
public void CalculateGravityVelocity_WhenPlayerIsNotMoving_
DecreasesPlayerYVelocity()
{
    float deltaTime = 1f;
    Vector3 playerOriginalVelocity = moveController.velocity;

    moveController.CalculateGravityVelocity(deltaTime);

    Assert.Less(moveController.velocity.y,
    playerOriginalVelocity.y);
```

```
    Assert.AreEqual(moveController.velocity.x,
    playerOriginalVelocity.x);
    Assert.AreEqual(moveController.velocity.z,
    playerOriginalVelocity.z);
    Assert.AreEqual(moveController.velocity.z, 0f);
}

[Test]
public void CalculateGravityVelocity_
WhenPlayerIsNotMovingAndDeltaTimeIsConsidered_
DecreasesPlayerYVelocity()
{
    float deltaTime = 0.3f;
    Vector3 playerOriginalVelocity = moveController.velocity;

    moveController.CalculateGravityVelocity(deltaTime);

    Vector3 playerGravityAppliedVelocity = moveController.
    velocity;

    Assert.That(Mathf.Approximately(playerGravityAppliedVelocit
    y.y, -2.94f));
    Assert.AreEqual(playerOriginalVelocity.y, 0f);
}
```
```

This can be fixed by multiplying gravity by deltaTime. See
Listing 16-65.
```

Listing 16-65. Calculating Gravity as a Time Dependent Property

```
```
public void CalculateGravityVelocity(float deltaTime)
{
    velocity.y += gravity * deltaTime;
}
```
```

Applying Gravity to Gameplay

If you try to play the game with the current changes, you will see that nothing happens, because you haven't actually applied the gravity effect to the character. To do this, you must first create a Play Mode test that checks if the player's position has decreased over time. See Listing 16-66.

Listing 16-66. Testing Position Change Based on Gravity

```
```
public class CharacterMovementTest
{
// ...
   [UnityTest]
    public IEnumerator ApplyGravity_AfterSeconds_
    MovesCubeDown()
    {
        GameObject go = new GameObject("Player");
        go.AddComponent<PlayerMovementController>();
        go.AddComponent<CharacterController>();
        go.AddComponent<UnityService>();
        Vector3 original = go.transform.position;
        PlayerMovementController moveController = go.Get
        Component<PlayerMovementController>();
```
```

```
        yield return new WaitForSeconds(0.05f);
        Vector3 actual = go.transform.position;

        Assert.AreNotEqual(original, actual);
        Assert.Less(actual.y, -0.5f);
        Assert.Greater(actual.y, -2.5f);
    }

}
```

Note that, for this test setting, as you are using UnityService and not FakeUnityService, the actual position is a range and not an exact value. This makes the test flaky, but is something nice to demonstrate. When you execute this test, notice that it fails. You need to implement an Update function that applies gravity (ApplyGravity), which calls Move on the character controller for the gravity velocity. See Listing 16-67.

Listing 16-67. Moving the Character Based on Gravity

```
public class PlayerMovementController : MonoBehaviour
{
    [SerializeField]
    public float xMovementSpeed = 20f;
    [SerializeField]
    public float yMovementSpeed = 35f;
    [SerializeField]
    public Vector3 velocity = Vector3.zero;
    float gravity = -9.8f;

  // ...

    void Update()
    {
```

```
    float horizontal = unityService.
    GetInputAxis("Horizontal");
    float vertical = unityService.GetInputAxis("Vertical");
    float deltaTime = unityService.GetDeltaTime();

    Vector3 movement = MovementOnX(horizontal, deltaTime) +
    MovementOnZ(vertical, deltaTime);

    controller.Move(movement);
    ApplyGravity(deltaTime);
    }

    void ApplyGravity(float deltaTime)
    {
    CalculateGravityVelocity(deltaTime);
    controller.Move(velocity);
    }

    public void CalculateGravityVelocity(float deltaTime)
    {
        velocity.y += gravity * deltaTime;
    }
    // ...
}
```

You need to remember that, although $V = Vo + g.t$, you are actually not calculating the relative motion of the character, $\Delta V = V - Vo$, but how much you are going to move the player to a new position, Δy. This is a different function, which is described by $\Delta y = \frac{1}{2} g . t\text{\textasciicircum}2$. This function means that the difference of position (Δy) is equal to the gravity (g) multiplied by delta time squared ($t\text{\textasciicircum}2$).

This is due to the fact that, although the character controller move function receives a motion as an argument, it is actually applying an absolute movement delta.[5] Considering this, one nice thing to have in this test is something to make sure that the distance is increasing with the square of time. You can do that by reducing the accepted position interval and adding the code block in Listing 16-68, which checks if the Δy in the second block is larger than twice the Δy in the first block. Add this to the previous test.

Listing 16-68. Δy Progression with Time Test

```
```
[UnityTest]
public IEnumerator ApplyGravity_AfterSeconds_MovesCubeDown()
{
    GameObject go = new GameObject("Player");
    go.AddComponent<PlayerMovementController>();
    go.AddComponent<CharacterController>();
    go.AddComponent<UnityService>();
    Vector3 original = go.transform.position;
    PlayerMovementController moveController = go.GetComponent<P
    layerMovementController>();

    yield return new WaitForSeconds(0.1f);
    Vector3 actual = go.transform.position;

    Assert.AreNotEqual(original, actual);
    Assert.Less(actual.y, -0.05f);
    Assert.Greater(actual.y, -0.08f);
```

---

[5] https://docs.unity3d.com/ScriptReference/CharacterController.Move.html
```

```
yield return new WaitForSeconds(0.1f);
Vector3 actual2 = go.transform.position;

Assert.AreNotEqual(actual, actual2);
Assert.Less(actual2.y, -0.2f);
Assert.Greater(actual2.y, -0.28f);
}
```

Note the increased wait time is now at 0.1, and the increased range for the first Δy is between 0.05 and 0.08 (which is less than half of the second Δy). This demonstrates the quadratic relationship. If you play the game now, gravity is applied but something seems weird, because the speed at which you go down seems to be increasing even when you are touching the ground. To fix that, a new test should be added to verify that when the character controller touches the ground, its speed is set to zero. The test in Listing 16-69 can help you check for that.

Listing 16-69. Tests if a Ground Touch Sets Gravity to Zero

```
[UnityTest]
public IEnumerator ApplyGravity_WehnHitsGround_VelocityIsZero()
{
    LayerMask groundMask = new LayerMask
    {
        value = 3
    };

    GameObject go = new GameObject("Player");
    go.AddComponent<PlayerMovementController>();
    go.AddComponent<CharacterController>();
    go.AddComponent<UnityService>();
```

```
PlayerMovementController moveController = go.GetComponent<P
layerMovementController>();
moveController.groundLayerMask = groundMask;
moveController.groundPosition = (new GameObject("Ground
position")).transform;

Vector3 original = go.transform.position;

GameObject ground = new GameObject("Ground");
ground.transform.localScale = new Vector3(100f, 1f, 100f);
ground.transform.position = Vector3.down * 3;
ground.AddComponent<BoxCollider>();
ground.layer = 3;

yield return new WaitForSeconds(3f);
Vector3 actual = go.transform.position;
Assert.Less(actual.y, original.y);
Assert.That(Mathf.Approximately(actual.y, -1.42f));
Assert.Less(-1.3f, moveController.velocity.y);
}
```

This test consists of a bunch of changes in PlayerMovementController.
The first change defines a position in the lower part of the character. The
second change defines a layer mask for detecting when the player collides
with the ground, then you need a "ground" game object to collide. After
yielding three seconds, there are three checks:

- Current position is lower than the original position,
  which means the object has fallen.

- Actual position is approximately floor position plus a
  detection sphere.

- When the player hits the ground, the velocity in y is less than a minimal velocity (-1f) added by Time. deltaTime.

Considering the current apply gravity scenario, when the test is executed, the velocity in the y axis is around -30f and if ground. AddComponent<BoxCollider>() is removed, the position of actual.y is much less than -10f. To solve this issue, a detection sphere should be added to the bottom of the player capsule, which will set the isGrounded flag to true when it hits the ground layer mask. Then, if the velocity is less than 0f and isGrounded is true, the velocity is set to near 0f. See Listing 16-70.

Listing 16-70. Implementing an isGrounded Check

```
```
public class PlayerMovementController : MonoBehaviour
{
    // ...
    [SerializeField]
    public Vector3 velocity = Vector3.zero;
    [SerializeField]
    public Transform groundPosition;
    public LayerMask groundLayerMask;

    float gravity = -9.8f;
    float detectionSphereRadius = 0.5f;
    bool isGrounded;

    void Start()
    {
        controller = GetComponent<CharacterController>();
        unityService = GetComponent<IUnityService>();
```
```

```
        groundPosition.position = transform.position -
        (Vector3.up * transform.localScale.y / 2);
    }

    void Update()
    {
        float horizontal = unityService.
        GetInputAxis("Horizontal");
        float vertical = unityService.GetInputAxis("Vertical");
        float deltaTime = unityService.GetDeltaTime();

        Vector3 movement = MovementOnX(horizontal, deltaTime) +
        MovementOnZ(vertical, deltaTime);

        controller.Move(movement);
        ApplyGravity(deltaTime);
    }

    void ApplyGravity(float deltaTime)
    {
        CalculateGravityVelocity(deltaTime);
        controller.Move(velocity * deltaTime);
    }

    public void CalculateGravityVelocity(float deltaTime)
    {
        isGrounded = Physics.CheckSphere(groundPosition.
        position, detectionSphereRadius, groundLayerMask);

        if (isGrounded && velocity.y < 0f)
        {
            velocity.y = -1f;
        } else
        {
```

```
        velocity.y += gravity * deltaTime;
    }
  }
// ...
}
```

Note that due to these changes, the other tests in CharacterMovementTest need to change as well. See Listing 16-71.

Listing 16-71. Compiled Test Scenarios

```
[UnityTest]
public IEnumerator CharacterMovement_When1SecondPassed_
MovesCharacter()
{
    LayerMask groundMask = new LayerMask
    {
        value = 0
    };
    GameObject go = new GameObject("Player");
    go.AddComponent<PlayerMovementController>();
    go.AddComponent<CharacterController>();
    go.AddComponent<FakeUnityService>();
    PlayerMovementController moveController = go.GetComponent<P
    layerMovementController>();
    moveController.groundLayerMask = groundMask;
    moveController.groundPosition = (new GameObject("Ground
    position")).transform;

    Vector3 original = go.transform.position;

    yield return new WaitForSeconds(0.1f);
```

```
    Vector3 actual = go.transform.position;

    Assert.AreNotEqual(original, actual);
}

[UnityTest]
public IEnumerator MovementAndRotation_OnRotatingView_
HasZXIncreasedInDifferentProportions()
{
    LayerMask groundMask = new LayerMask
    {
        value = 0
    };
    GameObject go = new GameObject("Player");
    go.AddComponent<PlayerMovementController>();
    go.AddComponent<CharacterController>();
    go.AddComponent<FakeUnityService>();
    go.AddComponent<Camera>();
    go.AddComponent<CameraMovementController>();
    PlayerMovementController moveController = go.GetComponent
    <PlayerMovementController>();
    moveController.groundLayerMask = groundMask;
    moveController.groundPosition = (new GameObject("Ground
    position")).transform;

    yield return new WaitForSeconds(0.1f);
    Vector3 origin = go.transform.position;

    yield return new WaitForSeconds(0.3f);

    Vector3 actual = go.transform.position;
    float xProportion = actual.x / origin.x;
    float zProportion = actual.z / origin.z;

    Assert.Greater(zProportion, xProportion);
```

```
}
[UnityTest]
public IEnumerator ApplyGravity_AfterSeconds_MovesCubeDown()
{
    LayerMask groundMask = new LayerMask
    {
        value = 0
    };
    GameObject go = new GameObject("Player");
    go.AddComponent<PlayerMovementController>();
    go.AddComponent<CharacterController>();
    go.AddComponent<UnityService>();
    PlayerMovementController moveController = go.GetComponent
    <PlayerMovementController>();
    moveController.groundLayerMask = groundMask;
    moveController.groundPosition = (new GameObject("Ground
    position")).transform;

    Vector3 original = go.transform.position;
    yield return new WaitForSeconds(0.1f);
    Vector3 actual = go.transform.position;

    Assert.AreNotEqual(original, actual);
    Assert.Less(actual.y, -0.05f);
    Assert.Greater(actual.y, -0.12f);

    yield return new WaitForSeconds(0.1f);
    Vector3 actual2 = go.transform.position;

    Assert.AreNotEqual(actual, actual2);
    Assert.Less(actual2.y, -0.22f);
    Assert.Greater(actual2.y, -0.33f);
}
```

```
[UnityTest]
public IEnumerator ApplyGravity_WehnHitsGround_VelocityIsZero()
{
    LayerMask groundMask = new LayerMask
    {
        value = 3
    };

    GameObject go = new GameObject("Player");
    go.AddComponent<PlayerMovementController>();
    go.AddComponent<CharacterController>();
    go.AddComponent<UnityService>();
    PlayerMovementController moveController = go.GetComponent
    <PlayerMovementController>();
    moveController.groundLayerMask = groundMask;
    moveController.groundPosition = (new GameObject("Ground
    position")).transform;

    Vector3 original = go.transform.position;

    GameObject ground = new GameObject("Ground");
    ground.transform.localScale = new Vector3(100f, 1f, 100f);
    ground.transform.position = Vector3.down * 3;
    ground.AddComponent<BoxCollider>();
    ground.layer = 3;

    yield return new WaitForSeconds(3f);
    Vector3 actual = go.transform.position;
    Assert.Less(actual.y, original.y);
    Assert.That(Mathf.Approximately(actual.y, -1.42f));
    Assert.Less(-1.3f, moveController.velocity.y);
}
```

```

```

As a next step, I suggest implementing the jumping code via TDD and submitting it to review in the project's GitHub.[6] You can open an issue or a pull request. And possibly, a double jump.

Summary

This chapter focused on strategies for writing code in a TDD manner, by writing Edit Mode tests to unitary functions and Play Mode tests to check gameplay. The tests focused on keyboard input, camera testing and rotation, as well as character movement and gravity.

---

[6] https://github.com/naomijub/FPSwithTDD

Index

© Julia Naomi Rosenfield Boeira 2024
J. N. Rosenfield Boeira, *Lean Game Development*,
https://doi.org/10.1007/978-1-4842-9843-5

H

Printed in the United States
by Baker & Taylor Publisher Services